Glimpses

in

Time:

A Collection of Memoirs and More.

Barbara Godin

D1500209

While every precaution has been taken in the preparation of this book, the publisher assumes no responsibility for errors or omissions, or for damages resulting from the use of the information contained herein.

GLIMPSES IN TIME: A COLLECTION OF MEMOIRS AND MORE

First edition. January 23, 2021.

ISBN: 978-1393038023

Written by BARBARA GODIN.

Table of Contents

Afterword | I hope you enjoyed reading this book. I would appreciate it if you could take the time to give me a rating or review on your favorite book site. | Feel free to send comments about this book or my previous book, Dear Barb: Answers to Your Everyday Questions- to my email at barbgodin53@gmail.com. | Follow my webpage barbgodin.com for the release of my next book and to read more of my writing. 147

About This Book

This book is a collection of memoirs and more that have been written over several years. Many of these articles have been previously published in *The Voice Magazine* www.voicemagazine.org.
Glimpses in Time is divided into three parts. Part 1 is memoirs. Part 2 is fiction stories and poetry. Part 3 is the first chapter in my unpublished autobiography, *Can I Come Home Now*?

Acknowledgements

This book would not have been possible without some very important people. First of all thank you to Paul Lima paullima.com for his assistance.

I would also like to express my gratitude to Barbara Lehtiniemi, a writer for *The Voice Magazine,* for her excellent proofreading skills.

A huge thank you to Karl Low, editor of *The Voice Magazine* for his expert editing skills and assistance in bringing many of these stories to publication.

Also I am forever indebted to Brenda Missen brendamissen.com who donated her writing and editing skills to a new author who was just starting out. Thank you for being my friend and helping me find my voice.

To my husband, who has always encouraged me and read and reread and reread my manuscripts, I am eternally grateful. Finally to my family, you know who you are, thank you for your support and encouragement.

Part 1

Memoirs

Miscellaneous
Nifty Fifty ... Maybe

AS I RELUCTANTLY APPROACHED my fiftieth birthday I wondered if turning fifty would really be as traumatic as I had heard. Fifty certainly did not feel or look like it did when I was thirty years old and looking ahead. However, the gray hair was real, as was the soft jaw line, among other things. I know I eat pretty well the same quantity of food as I have for as long as I can remember, but it is becoming more difficult to keep that "girlish figure." By the way, has someone turned up the heat? Maybe it is global warming, but everywhere I go I feel so much warmer than I used to, even to the point of spontaneously breaking out in a sweat with no physical effort.

Though being a grandmother fits in with the stereotypical fifty year old, or should I say "middle-ager," I am also working toward my university degree. This was not a common occurrence 20 years ago, but it now seems to be happening more frequently in the over forty age group. Perhaps this is the baby boomers way of trying to catch up on what we missed, during the drug culture of our youth.

Against the urging of family and friends that I must have a party – a huge party, big celebration, rent a hall, go on a trip – April 6, came and went fairly inconspicuously. A small party with family and friends and I became a middle-age baby-boomer, joining so many of my cohorts already basking in the glow of acquired wisdom.

Only months into my new era, I was beginning to feel different. Hey I'm 50; I don't have to make excuses because my waistline isn't like that of my 29-year-old daughter, or try to compete with the Susan Lucci's of daytime TV. I don't need surgery or Botox. I'm proud of that wiry gray hair that sticks straight out, as if having a mind of its own.

Most importantly, I don't feel I have to please everyone else, or aspire to make everyone like me. Nor do I have to put my dreams on hold while helping others carve their path in life. Now I can cultivate pleasing myself. I can give myself permission to fulfill my own dreams and strive to make the rest of my life happy. Becoming 50 has allowed me the permission to finally accept myself without apologies. Turning 50 is all right!

The Absurdity of Camping

AS THE CAMPING SEASON draws to a close for another year, I feel somewhat saddened. I will miss those days spent getting in touch with nature. I will definitely miss those hot humid days with no air conditioning, watching the bugs swarming around my food and ultimately dropping into my cool glass of wine. I will yearn for those morning lineups at the shower, waiting to get into a stall that will be peppered with unknown items, which I am glad I don't have to clean.

"Camping breakfasts" are the best. Nothing compares to greasy fried eggs and bacon, done over a propane stove. Morning coffee is a necessity – fresh brewed, with water from a questionable source. I will undeniably miss those mornings.

During the long winter I will yearn for those leisurely days spent, biking, hiking and swimming, all the while trying wholeheartedly to keep ahead of the bugs. Slathers of greasy sun screen is a necessity, thus attracting additional swarms of deer flies, regular flies and any other variety of winged varmint. Hence requiring a further coating of bug repellent, containing deet, which, however, can only safely be applied every six hours, but the varmints are back within three. Oh well.

What can be more enjoyable than a barbeque? Camping and barbeques go together – juicy red sirloin steaks grilling on an open flame. So what if they've found carcinogens in the smoke from barbequing meat. If the flames get too high, we just lift the steaks off the grill and wave them around until the blaze subsides – or simply beat them down with a wooden spatula. Even charred black meat tastes good after a day outdoors.

Camping is a family affair, so of course we have to take our dog and cat. Ahhh, nothing like the smell of a wet dog inside a hot, stifling tent trailer. Of course Boots, being the attack cat that she is, spends her days batting at bugs or throwing cat litter all over the trailer. Her evenings include running from one end of the trailer to the other, chasing bugs that only she can see, and jumping on whatever, or whoever, is in her pathway. Our evenings are joyously spent coughing and gagging as the smoke from neighbouring campfires fills our trailer.

Sadly, I guess I'll just have to adapt to spending my evenings in front of the warm cozy fireplace, sipping wine and munching on crackers and cheese, until camping seasons begins again.

Trip to Branson

MY HUSBAND AND I DECIDED to go on a road trip this year for our twentieth anniversary. We wanted to do something that would be memorable. We'd been to the Canadian east coast and didn't want to go to the west coast, so where could we go?

I always wanted to go to Memphis, to see Graceland. I'm not a big Elvis fan, but thought I'd like to go there. Ed wasn't too keen on it. Where else could we go? How about Branson, Missouri? We'd seen many entertainers on *Larry King Live* and various other entertainment shows, discussing their acts in Branson, Missouri. I looked up the web site. "*Go ahead fulfill a dream, laugh out loud, get your feet wet, reach for the stars, go for adventure in Branson, Missouri.*" Okay I'm ready for that. We decided that yes, we were going to Branson Missouri.

We bought tickets online to a couple of live shows, booked a campsite and were ready to go. When we told family and friends where we were going, we were met with surprised looks, "I didn't know you were country and western fans." "Well we're not really; there are lots of other things to do in Branson – I think."

Upon starting out I didn't realize how far 930 miles really is. We decided to take two days to get there. Since we had our cat and dog with us we would need to stop frequently; we can't leave them at home, they are part of the family and they really are good travelers.

Well, by the time we got to Terre Haute, Indiana, we were tired, hungry and just a wee bit miserable. After regrouping and having a good night's sleep, we were off again for our second day. We saw lots of sights along the highway, for example three dead deer, one with a large dog standing over it looking like someone who won first prize in a pie-eating contest. We also saw a truck with the cab in flames, as well as a few rollovers.

The most intimidating aspect of driving the Interstate Highways in the States and the 400 series in Canada is the trucks. Fortunately, my husband is a good driver. He only nearly killed us once, when he decided not to let a truck enter the lane in front of us, but ultimately he decided that wasn't a good idea.

Driving into Branson is amazing. For miles and miles there are signs advertising who is performing, as well as all the activities, like shopping etc. Several colorful billboards announced *"Ann Margaret and Andy Williams performing together again."* I must admit I didn't remember them performing together previously. Nonetheless we would not be able to see them as they were opening the day we were to leave. The weather was gorgeous, 85 degrees and sunny. The campground we stayed at was in the Ozark Mountains and the campsites were strategically layered into the mountainside. We were able to pick our campsite when we arrived on a Monday in late April: definitely not peak tourist season. In fact I would estimate there were approximately 15 campers in a campground that could easily accommodate hundreds.

Our first day was spent touring, shopping, going to the Wax Museum, and a most nostalgic trip through the Toy Museum. The countryside was breathtaking. On our second day, as we returned to our campsite around dinnertime, we noticed the sky darkening. We had a good day and didn't mind if it rained a little. As we watched the local news, a red flashing warning came across the screen, TORNADO WATCH FOR FAYETTEVILLE COUNTY AND THE ARKANSAS BORDER AREA. Is that us? We knew we were close to the Arkansas border, so we got out the map. Yes that was fairly close. We continued to watch the news as the tornado watch turned into a warning and included our county. I was a little concerned, or should I say a lot concerned, as the rain poured, the winds blew and the thunder rolled for most of the night. Thoughts raced through my mind: what if the winds picked us up and dropped us down the mountainside? I tried to push those thoughts out of my mind as I listened to Ed's rhythmic breathing, seeming to not have a care in the world.

Fortunately none of my fears came true, as we awoke still in one piece in our wet, humid trailer. That day we talked to others at the campground; "Well, this is tornado season." I turned to Ed with a surprised look, his response was casual, "Well, we are near Kansas, you know what happened to Dorothy and Toto." I did not think that was funny. For the next six nights, after enjoying days filled with new adventures, I would lay in our camper in the Ozark Mountains, waiting to be blown away, wishing I could just click my heels and be home.

One morning we awoke to hear that a tornado had touched down in Illinois and had flattened a bar, which was full of people from a nearby campground. The victims felt they would be safer in the bar than at the campground. Fortunately no one was seriously injured.

In spite of everything our days filled with shows, shopping, theme parks, outdoor theaters and perfect weather, compensated nicely for our nights, which were a wee bit scary for a person who is rather fearful of a regular thunderstorm. Nonetheless I would not hesitate to return to Branson, Missouri — just not during tornado season!

A Special Christmas Memory

AS MY HUSBAND AND I decorated our Christmas tree, my mind trailed off to past years, especially one particular Christmas with my mom. Although I didn't know it at the time, this would be the last Christmas day that I ever remember spending with my mom. I was a young girl, maybe eight or nine years old and living in a small house with my mom and her boyfriend. We didn't have a lot, but that didn't matter; my heart was ready to burst because I was with my mom for Christmas. I couldn't remember any other Christmases with Mom and I knew this would be a special one. My siblings were all living with different family members and I would not see them this year, but I was overjoyed to spend this Christmas with my mom.

On Christmas Eve mom's boyfriend, John, brought a little Christmas tree home for us to decorate. He set up the tree and mom and I dug out some decorations from her closet. I was anxious to open the old yellowed boxes. They were filled with red and green shiny, glittery bulbs. Mom carefully attached the hooks through the loops and handed them to me to hang on the tree. After the bulbs were all on the tree, mom handed me a special decoration. It was a little elf with long red legs and a pointy hat. I loved it and hung it right in the front centre of the tree. Mom and I laughed together. I hardly ever heard mom laugh and I felt a catch in my throat as she put her arms around me. I was so happy I felt I was going to explode. I hoped I would be able to stay with mom forever.

While we were decorating the tree, mom kept looking out the front window onto the porch as if she was waiting for something. From my bedroom I heard her say to John, "It's here." I came out to see what it was. John was carrying in a basket filled with stuff. I could see what looked like a turkey on top. Mom quickly went through the basket while I watched. Then she handed me a wrapped present and asked me to put it under the tree. As I carried it I peeked at the name tag and it said "To: Barbara." I was so excited. I asked mom if I could open it and she said not until morning. That evening mom and I sat on the sofa and watched *Miracle on 34th Street*. I loved spending time with mom, I felt so loved and special. After the movie, mom tucked me in bed and I quickly fell asleep.

The next morning, I ran into the living room and saw two more gifts. I woke up mom and she said I could open the gifts. I saved the biggest one for last. I tore open the wrapping and there was a beautiful walking doll! This was the best gift of all. Afterward, mom sat with me on the sofa and I placed the doll between us. Mom prepared a Christmas dinner with turkey, potatoes, and stuffing, my favorite. That evening as I said goodnight, I hugged mom tightly and whispered in her ear. "I love you mom, I had the best Christmas ever." She looked into my eyes and I could see the tears filling her eyes as she hugged me closely. I wondered why she was crying.

That summer I was sent for a visit with friends of the family. It was supposed to be a two-week visit, but I ended up staying there for many years. I missed my mom every day, but especially at Christmas. As the years passed that one Christmas day with my mom will always be a magical memory for me.

My New Year's Resolution

NEW YEAR'S DAY IS TRADITIONALLY seen as a new beginning, providing an opportunity to change bad habits and improve our lifestyle. For example, we can aim to overcome shyness, become more assertive – ask for that raise, become more social, more tolerant of others, less judgmental, any number of choices are available to us. Perhaps New Year's gives us the belief that, at least for one day, we are able to choose the course of our lives from this day forward. I read somewhere that the average person makes one and a half New Year's resolutions each year. The most common resolutions are losing weight, exercising more and quitting smoking. How successful these one and a half resolutions are, is anybody's guess.

What will my New Year's resolution be for this year? I think I'll try choosing something that I can stick with, maybe that way I will feel better about myself at the end of the year, and feel that I really did accomplish something.

Let me see...quit smoking, no...been there done that. Losing weight? Okay let's be realistic, am I really going to stick to a diet or exercise plan, and do I really need or want to lose weight? After all I don't look too bad, for my age that is. Okay two down, what else? Perhaps being less frivolous with my spending. I guess I do shop more than I need to, but is this something I can live with..."not shopping?" But what about that special party? I'll have to buy a new dress. What about my spring wardrobe? Of course I have to have new clothes, or at least a new bathing suit. Naw, that's not a good resolution, I'd only be setting myself up for failure. Keeping with this theme, maybe I should contribute more to my RRSP, after all "they" keep telling us we haven't saved enough for retirement. Okay maybe I can contribute monthly, but can I afford it? What about living now? What if I don't live to retirement, then I will have deprived myself for nothing. Maybe I need to give this a little more thought.

On the more practical side, I could resolve to finally organize my closets and kitchen cupboards, followed by a huge garage sale. That's a plan – the money from the garage sale could go into my RRSP. Okay, I can feel the stress building already. When will I have the time to do this? I know it will take longer than one day; after all, I have five closets and umpteen kitchen cupboards. I will check out the calendar... no, not this week, forget February, maybe in March. It would have to be done before summer cause that's when camping starts. In September I plan to take another course, so that will keep me pretty busy until Christmas. Oh well, maybe that's not a good resolution. On to the next one.

There's got to be something I know I can commit to doing. How about learning something new? Well, I do take courses and I am already working toward my degree, could I really commit to doing more than that... I don't think so. Okay what else... can't think of anything.

After much thought I think I've finally found one I can stick to. My New Year's resolution for 2004 will be to become a more tolerant and accepting individual, beginning with myself and my limited ability to actualize my New Year's resolutions.

The Changing Family

NOW THAT I HAVE REACHED the mature age of fifty plus, I wonder about the word "family." In today's society, the word family conjures up many more images than it did in the 1960s when my family began its gradual disintegration. As a result of this new version of family, I believe there will be fewer scarred individuals 50 years from now.

When meeting a family unit consisting of what appears to be a mother, father and two or three children, one cannot really be sure if this is a biological family. It could consist of any number of different scenarios. For example, the children could belong to either parent, or each child could belong to one parent. Perhaps the children are adopted, or maybe only one is adopted. Are the parents married or cohabitating? Maybe they are just friends sharing the same home for economic reasons. Also, many children today are raised by grandparents. I could go on and on. The bottom line is, for the most part, today's society is accepting of a much broader definition of family than it was 50 years ago.

Back in the "olden days" when I was growing up, the only acceptable family was the traditional, biological family. As a result of my parents' divorce, my three siblings and I grew up being ashamed of our family and rarely chose to bring friends home. Through most of my school years, I was the only one in my classroom that had divorced parents. At school concerts, or other activities where parents were invited, I almost became physically ill thinking about my parents attending. I would often "forget" to tell my mother about school events. What made the situation even worse was that my mother was cohabitating with a man. Living with a man to whom you were not married was completely taboo in the late 1950s and early 1960s. If my mother brought this man to school events, it would be even worse for me. How would I explain his presence to my friends and even my teachers? Everyone would know he wasn't my father, because my father had been at the school to pick me up. My friends had met my father, but I failed to tell them that he did not live with us.

At other times in my life, I lived with my grandparents who were wonderful people. They attended school concerts and parent/teacher interviews, and the following day I would have to face a barrage of questions from classmates, as well as the accompanying looks confirming what I already knew; there really was something wrong with me. Even worse were the looks of pity. "Were my parents dead?" they would ask. "No," I would reply. "-"Well, why don't you live with them?"

Even forty some years later, I can still feel the sting of growing up in a family that did not fit into society's definition. As times change, many lifestyles that are considered unacceptable and taboo today, for example gay marriages, will become just another lifestyle choice in the future.

Something to think about.

A Man's Legacy

THE LEGACY A MAN LEAVES for his children is precious. It took many years for me to heal the scars left from damaging father figures. Despite the negatives, life always provides us with a counteracting positive, if we only allow ourselves to see it.

Each man in my life has taught me something about life—some good, some not so good—beginning with my biological father. When I think about my dad I feel love, and loss, both at the same time. Dad was a reserved Englishman who rarely showed affection to any of his four children. He was a heavy drinker. I don't really recall him being drunk or doing anything irrational, but that's not to say he didn't—I just didn't see it. I loved the part of him where I could see reflections of myself, and I knew we were a part of each other. For example, we both had a short big toe, which is an inherited condition called Morton's Syndrome.

My parents divorced when I was one and a half years old, so my father was in and out of my life. I lived with him for a short time and I have only good memories of that time. But along with the good memories there is emptiness, as I don't feel I really knew him. The best word to describe my feelings for my dad was "composed." There was nothing intense, and I didn't miss him when I didn't see him. When I visited, we just sat together, exchanging few words. He didn't attend my wedding. And that was okay with me.

I learned from my dad that you can love someone just because of the place they hold in your life.

After my parents separated, Mom met John, a convicted rapist, in a bar and brought him into her children's lives. He was a man that you could easily describe as "creepy." He barely talked above a whisper and had a sinister laugh, which always made me feel as if I had done something wrong. He did terrible things to my sister, things that she never was able to get over, things that you only read about in books. I will always remember the dark green blinds in our house that were kept tightly closed, as John was always fearful someone was after him. He systematically forced my mother to choose between him and her children, and, for the most part, she chose him. However, for some reason, he seemed to like me. At the time I was happy that I was able to stay with mom, I loved her so much. Up until that point she was the constant in my life. But as mom and John's relationship deteriorated, and the fighting escalated, I began to wish I was somewhere else. Their relationship was filled with fighting and horrible name calling and the police were constantly at our door. John's uncle and his wife, who had no children, began taking me to their place for weekends. As my life was becoming filled with fear I looked forward to spending the weekends at their home.

John taught me that sometimes it's easier to just play the game.

My weekend visits to the Russell's eventually turned into year-long visits. At first, I liked it there; it was quiet and everything seemed normal like other kids homes, but things changed. Aunt Alice was a harsh, strict woman who always seemed to have health problems and spent most of her time lying on the sofa. I tried to get along with her, but I felt such anger toward her because she was trying to be a mother to me, and I already had a mother. Often Uncle George stepped in and tried to smooth things over. He was very nice to me and took me everywhere with him. He was the father figure I missed and he became like a real dad to me. I loved him and I believed he loved me. But very quickly his vision of love became twisted and sick, and every day I just wished I could leave there.

He taught me not to trust, as people are often not who they appear to be.

As soon as I was able to, I moved out on my own. I met and married my first husband. We were two dysfunctional teenagers, trying to escape unhappy homes. We had not finished high school and were working at minimum wage jobs, which inevitably led to financial stress. When our daughter was born the stress only escalated. We argued constantly about everything. We had some happy times with our daughter, but ultimately drugs and abuse caused me to take my daughter and escape.

From my first husband I learned that no one else can make you whole, it has to come from within.

My second husband was my lifeline. He restored my faith in men. He loved me unconditionally and always assured me that everything would be fine. He took care of my every need.

It was as if his whole purpose in life was to make me happy. At first I found it difficult to accept that life really can be this happy and people can be trusted. I relentlessly tested Ed to make sure he wasn't going to be like the other men in my life, and he never crumbled. We experienced the normal ups and downs that couples go through, but, our life was largely bliss. I thought my life would always be like that until the fateful day when cancer entered our lives.

One year later my dream was over and life was forever changed. My heart was broken. All the pain from the past flooded forward. It took a long time to be able to feel past the pain and see the precious gift I had been given.

Ed taught me that I am lovable and worthy of being loved.

I truly believed Ed was the last man who would be a part of my life, until I met Stan. He had also lost his wife, and through our shared grief we began a relationship. Stan and I healed our grief together and could understand and share the deep pain of losing a loved one. Although Stan grew up without a father, he overcame and was a truly amazing father to his sons.

Stan showed me, and continues to show me, the true meaning of the word father.

20 Things

NEW YEAR'S IS A TIME of reflection, so as I was reflecting I thought I'd write down some of my thoughts.

20 Things I've Learned in Life

1. There are people you can trust and people you can't, the important thing is to know the difference.

2. Everyone is on their own personal journey, some you can understand and some you just wonder why?

3. Soul mates don't have to be a spouse; they can be a friend, sibling, co-worker etc.

4. Parents don't always love their children and children don't always love their parents.

5. What goes around doesn't always come around.

6. Grief never ends; it's just hidden till the next trigger.

7. You can have more than one true love.

8. Some people would rather be right than happy.

9. Compassion and empathy are not present in every person.

10. People who want to be in your life will be.

11. Some people hold grudges their whole lives, never realizing they are hurting themselves.

12. Death comes calling whether you want it or not.

13. You can love a pet as much as a person.

14. Grandchildren show us that we can love someone else's child as much as our own.

15. Life isn't always fair.

16. Love is the universal language.

17. Hate is evil and destructive at any level

18. Words are the only way to heal an injured relationship.

19. There is a higher power that we don't truly understand.

20. Once a relationship is severed it can never be fully repaired.

Grief
Mary's Story

THE FOLLOWING STORY was awarded first place in the 2019 short article category from the **Professional Writers Association of Canada***, now the* **Canadian Freelance Guild** *https://canadianfreelanceguild.ca/en/*

MARY AND I SPENT PART of our childhood together. She was my closest sibling, and I always felt we were a part of each other. I was connected to Mary in a way that I wasn't with my other siblings, or even my parents. We shared the pain of being born into a family where we felt totally unwanted and experienced abuse and neglect.

As teenagers, Mary and I were involved in a deadly car accident where a friend was killed. Mary sustained a traumatic brain injury and numerous other injuries including a broken leg and pelvis. My injuries were minimal. The brain injury changed Mary and our relationship forever. I tried many times over the years to reconnect with her but it was always strained. We grew more distant, only writing at Christmas or birthdays. We both married and had children, but our families hardly knew each other.

During the last five years of Mary's life things changed and we began to talk more. I soon began to realize how ill Mary was, both physically and mentally. I was shocked to see the transformation from the last time I had seen her. She had no teeth, did not wear dentures, and was extremely thin. Her spine was twisted with osteoporosis, making it impossible for her to stand straight. She often lost her balance and fell, usually hitting her head.

My heart ached for Mary. I hated the pain she was living with and I wanted her life to be better. She weighed between 75 and 80 pounds and her diet consisted mainly of Cheerios, peanut butter, diet Coke and black coffee which she ordered from the neighborhood convenience store since they delivered. She slept 18 hours a day. If I called her before 7 or 8 in the evening she was in such a deep sleep that her phone would ring so long that the operator came on. Her mental state continued to deteriorate. She was irrational and suffered from temporal lobe seizures and rages.

The osteoporosis had been brought on because the medication she was taking for seizures had depleted her bones of calcium. It could have been prevented if her doctor had put her on calcium supplements, but neither Mary's doctor nor the pharmacist told her this was a side effect. In fact, the situation only came to the doctor's attention when our older sister took Mary for a doctor's appointment and mentioned the curvature in her back. She was sent for a bone density test and the diagnosis was made, and then she was prescribed calcium supplements. Mary took the medication, but she refused to accept that she had osteoporosis, nor would she agree to use a walker or cane to help with her balance.

Following a fall and a visit to the hospital, the hospital refused to discharge Mary unless she agreed to use a walker. She agreed, reluctantly, but two days after leaving the hospital she called the pharmacy and told them to pick up the walker, which was sitting outside her apartment door. I tried to convince her to keep it but her response was "I'm only a year older than you and you don't have one."

Mary's mental illness was extremely frustrating. She saw everyone as a threat. She told me people were coming into her apartment and stealing her cigarettes and diet Coke, and leaving notes that she would find posted on her fridge. I tried to explain to her that no one could get in with her door locked and the chain and knives across it. She was convinced we were trying to put her in a home, when, in reality, we were trying to get her some help to improve her life.

One evening, after we talked on the phone and had a good conversation, or so I thought, she reported me to the police. I was awakened at midnight to the sound of my phone ringing. The police officer on the other end of the line said he had received a complaint from Mary that I had been harassing her. She regularly blocked my number and I was not able to call her for months. Then, out of the blue, she would call and ask why I had blocked her. I was angry, frustrated, and almost ready to give up. During her lucid times we talked about the pain and betrayal we felt from being abandoned by our parents. We knew how each other felt and I made the decision to always be there for Mary. Every time I spoke to her, she asked me to tell her daughter that she loved her and I promised her that I would. At times I believed I was reaching her and that she was ready to accept help, but she never did.

I had not physically seen Mary for two years before her death, but I knew she was getting worse when she told me her physical symptoms. She described cuts and bruises she had gotten from falling and said that her fingers and toes were black. She said everything she ate went right through her and left her toilet full of blood. I feared for her and made her promise to tell her social worker. At times family members had contacted her doctor and social worker, but with the privacy laws, there was nothing anyone could do without Mary agreeing to accept help. I lived in another city a two-hour drive away and when we made plans to visit, she always cancelled. Eventually her children, grandchildren, and our other sister grew tired and frustrated from the abusive rages she'd direct toward them and they stopped contacting her.

The last time I talked to her was in June 2017, six weeks before she died. We had a great conversation and made plans for me to visit the next week. I went shopping and purchased a few items to bring for our visit. The day before the visit, I called and a recording came on: "This person is not accepting calls from you at the present time." I called on my cell phone and she seemed confused as to how I was able to call her. She cancelled our visit and banged the phone down. I decided to give it a few weeks and call her again, but that would never happen.

A couple of weeks later we went camping for the weekend. On Friday afternoon, after parking and setting up our camper, I received a call from Mary's social worker, Nadia. She said that Mary had been admitted to the hospital with pneumonia. Nadia said Mary was not doing well and she had lost more weight, and her mental and physical health was getting worse. She said that we needed to get together as a family and have

Mary moved into to an assisted living facility, because the hospital might decide to only release her if she went into an assisted living facility. But if the hospital chose to release her on her own, our next step was to go before a judge and have her declared incapable of taking care of herself. We did not want to take Mary's independence away, but it seemed there was no other option as she was getting worse. We decided that if the hospital sent her home we would begin the legal proceeding immediately. On Saturday morning I called the hospital from the campground, hoping to be able to talk to Mary, but they said she had been discharged. I was surprised, but, in a way, I was relieved that they felt she was well enough to be released.

Two days later when I returned home Mary's social worker called and told me that Mary had passed away. I was confused and thought she must be mistaken. Nadia said the hospital had misinformed me and Mary had never been discharged. She died a few hours after being admitted as a result of the pneumonia. Mary had no one listed as next of kin; therefore no one was informed of her passing. She died all alone in a hospital bed with no one by her side. My heart broke for her having to spend the last minutes of life alone. I didn't want this horrible end for Mary. I wanted to be with her, to help her heal the pain. My chest felt tight, I did not want to breathe in this reality. My eyes burned with tears.

A part of me died that day with my sister. I think about her every day and wonder why she had to live such a tortured life. She was a menace to herself and the only people who could help her, let her down. Her doctors, social workers and family should have been able to save Mary from herself, but because of the mental health act, there was nothing anyone could do without her consent. Mary was never able to find peace while alive. Happiness came to her only in glimpses.

Goodnight My Love

HE SAT IN THE CORNER of the room, looking out the window. From his hospital bed he could see the crimson leaves waiting to drop to the ground. It was late fall and he knew this would be his last season on this earth. Though he struggled to hang on, his life was slipping away.

As the familiar footsteps grew louder, closer, he knew his wife was here for her daily visit. He hated to put her through this. She smiled as she saw the frail, shrivelled body of the man she had loved for the last 25 years. She also knew his life was slipping away. She sat on the bed and asked how he felt.

"Pretty good."

She knew he would say that; he always did, even after the rounds of chemo and the blasts of radiation, he never complained. Sometimes it made her frustrated, even angry. She wished he would tell her how he felt—cry, yell, share his pain with her. He didn't want her to be concerned. How could she not be concerned? The doctor told her he only had "days to weeks" left. That was three days ago.

They sat together talking about nothing, though every word would become etched in her mind for eternity.

"Help me."

"What do you need?"

"I want to go home."

"You can't, the doctor said you need to be here."

He looked away from her. They both knew he would never go home. They had talked about it, but hoped they had more time.

"I'm tired."

"I know."

"I'm going to lie down."

"I'll help you."

She held his tubes and IV lines while he got comfortable. He looked into her eyes.

"Will I be all right?"

"Yes, they'll take good care of you here."

She sat beside him holding his warm hand as he closed his eyes. She thought of a short time ago when his hand held hers and they walked together in the woods near their home. She remembered how he gently caressed her feet as they lay in his lap each evening while they sat together watching television or talking and sharing their dreams for the future. These were the hands that gently touched her as they made love.

His breathing changed. She touched his brow and kissed his soft lips.

"Good night, my sweet gentle husband."

Ray

RAY WAS MY BROTHER-in-law for over fifty years. He passed away on my birthday. When I heard he was in the hospital and things were not looking good I kept thinking, "not on my birthday, I don't want to have to live with this memory."

Ray was a special person. I know everyone says that about someone after they pass away, but Ray truly was a special person. I cannot remember a time when Ray was not a part of my life. Ray and my sister genuinely had a remarkable love. One which produced four children and numerous grandchildren. I didn't pay much attention to Ray while I was growing up; he was just the guy that everyone liked. He had a big presence and a bigger voice, and his hugs made you feel all warm and cozy. Ray made everyone he met feel they mattered to him and every person who met Ray remembered him, even if they only met him once. He always wore his signature red shirt and was often seen with a Tim Hortons coffee in hand.

When I began writing he often critiqued my stories and more often than not played the devil's advocate with my *Dear Barb* column, a weekly advice column in *The Voice Magazine*. If Ray suggested an alternate answer it frequently gave me pause to reconsider. A couple of times Ray even sent questions in to *The Voice*. Ray and I had verbal sparring matches, but they never became serious or hostile. We shared a mutual respect. Ray wasn't the type of person you could get angry at, as his heart was in the right place. His love for his family was enormous and it was mutual.

As he began to physically decline, no one wanted to see it. He had been losing weight and had been having dizzy spells. He was hospitalized on a couple of occasions and diagnosed with having mini strokes. He seemed to come through them with no ill effects and quickly returned to being "Uncle Ray", as he was affectionately known. My heart broke when my sister called me the night before my birthday to tell me Ray had collapsed and was in the hospital, diagnosed with a brain bleed. He peacefully fell into a deep sleep and passed away the following day with family and friends gathered around.

Ray's funeral was huge, with hundreds of people attending and sharing all their special memories with my sister. In the time since he passed, I think about him most days. I know he would have been proud that I won first place from the Professional Writers Association of Canada for a story, congratulating me with one of his bear hugs. Ray was my brother-in-law, but he always felt more like a brother to me. I will always miss our special times filled with laughter and love. Ray possessed a unique gift that anyone would be grateful to have, and he will be remembered by all who knew him. My birthday will always be a bittersweet day, as my heart will be heavy with memories of the loss of my dear brother.

Josh's Story

MY GREAT-NEPHEW JOSH was just twenty-seven years old when his young life tragically ended. Josh was a popular, friendly guy who would do anything to help a friend. He could always be found in his garage rebuilding Jeeps, trucks, or other vehicles. Josh's father, Mike, and sister, Jenn, were attempting to heal and recover from the devastating loss of their beloved wife and mother as a result of a car accident two years earlier. Recently, Josh had met and fallen in love with Melissa, and he was finally able to envision a bright future for him and his young daughter, Aaliyah (Bee). But everything changed on the morning of July 15, 2016, when Josh jumped on his newly purchased Suzuki motorcycle and began the half hour drive to his job. Disaster struck. A horrific crash found him being rushed to a nearby hospital in critical condition. It was bad enough that the *Windsor Star* reported on it[1].

Mike and Jenn arrived at the hospital and were assured by the attending nurse that Josh would survive, although the road to recovery would be long and difficult. But within hours Josh's condition deteriorated as his brain began to swell. After many attempts to stop the swelling the doctors stopped offering hope for recovery. There was no brain activity. Life support was the

---

1. http://windsorstar.com/news/local-news/

motorcyclist-in-fatal-ojibway-parkway-crash-was-a-safe-rider-say-friends only thing keeping Josh alive. Mike and Jenn knew this was not the life Josh would have wanted, but as they stood in the hall trying to digest the fact that they would have to face another loss, Josh's nurse asked to meet with them. Mike knew they were going to ask about organ donation and his immediate response was "no," he was not going to donate his son's organs. Jenn, on the other hand, was an organ donor. She shared with her dad her belief that if Josh were in their shoes, he would say "go for it." Mike was still hesitant, but when Jenn mentioned their late mother, who had been a nurse and would have wanted to help others, Mike knew in his heart it was the right thing to do. The heart wrenching decision was made. Arrangements were put in place, recipients were notified, and, on July 19, 2016, Jenn and Mike said a final goodbye to their beloved son and brother.

Ten days later Mike and Jenn received a letter from the Trillium Gift of Life Network thanking them for being an organ donor. Four people with terminal medical conditions had been helped according to the letter. At this point, Mike and Jenn knew that, as painful as it had been, they had made the right decision. Since Josh's passing, his family continues to receive anonymous personal letters from thankful recipients. Following are some excerpts from two of the letters they received. The first one is from a kidney and pancreas recipient.

"I am the recipient of your family member's two organs, kidney and pancreas. I am an elementary school teacher and have had diabetes for many years and developed kidney disease as a complication. The thought of being rid of both diseases was a miracle in my eyes. I have been struggling in writing this letter to you because I can't express my gratitude enough. How do you say thank you enough to a family that has suffered such a great loss. The impact this transplant has had on me has had its ups and downs, only because I am so grateful for the gift you have given me and also feel so compassionately about what you have gone through. I want to thank you from the bottom of my heart and most sincerely for giving the gift of life and giving me, personally, a second chance at life! You are truly a blessing."

And an excerpt from a letter sent by the recipient of Josh's lungs

"Thank you! Thank you! Thank you! Such small words that hold so much heartfelt meaning. I can't even begin to express the joy and happiness I have in my heart because of you and your loved one's generous gift. My family and I are so blessed and grateful to you knowing I will be able to live a longer and healthier life. I can play and watch my grandchildren grow. I can travel and go camping once again. How great it is to be able to just stand and take in a deep breath and smell the fresh-fallen rain and to walk more than 300 meters without running out of air. My life was not much more than just existing. We prayed for a miracle and then that day came, our prayers were answered. The gift of your loved one was given to me and gave me a second chance at life. I am looking forward to a brighter future. So thank you once again. I am so grateful to you and I promise I will do everything possible to live with great care, responsibility, healthy habits and love life to the fullest, to honor you and your loved one. "

Mike still has his hesitations about organ donation, but he appreciates that his son could give others a chance at life. No matter how painful it is for Jenn to read these letters, she knows

Josh is at peace knowing he could help others right through to the end of his life. She remains a strong supporter of organ donation and encourages others to sign their donor card.

Rusty's Gift

EVERY SUNDAY MORNING, without fail, my husband and I drove to our local Humane Society and walked the dogs. I walked the small ones and Ed walked the larger ones. Some days all the cages were full and other days there would be only one or two lonely, scraggly dogs. Little did I know that one Sunday morning my life would be changed forever.

It was Labor Day weekend and after we completed walking the dogs and were ready to go home, one of the staff members came rushing towards us. "Barb, I have to ask you guys a big favor. I have a little pup that someone dropped off and it's too young to leave at the shelter overnight, and tomorrow is a holiday so we'll only be coming in briefly to feed and clean cages. Would you and Ed be able to shelter this pup for a few days?" I looked at Ed and we both agreed. She ran to the back and brought out the cutest little blonde pup I had ever seen. I held her while Michelle handed Ed the food along with a bed and blanket. We headed home with the hope that our dog and cat would accept this pup without too much chaos and they did.

We soon discovered the pup was covered in fleas! Also, when I took her out to pee I thought she had eaten spaghetti, as long white strings were exiting her back end, but on a closer look I realized she was infested with worms. I was almost sick to my stomach. This poor little pup. And there was nothing we could do until Tuesday, as no one was at the shelter. We tried unsuccessfully to keep the pup away from our pets, but they were all too curious. Fleas were everywhere! I thought, "Well it's only a couple of days. We'll get through this." Unfortunately, overnight the pup started vomiting and having bloody diarrhea. Oh my goodness, what else can happen!

We had no choice but to bring her into the Emergency Veterinary Clinic. She was diagnosed with the parvo virus, which they explained was a very serious, life-threatening condition and she needed to be started on IV fluids immediately. The next day we called the Humane Society and told them the situation. Michelle asked if we could bring her back as they couldn't afford to keep her at the clinic and they would be able to hydrate her at the shelter. When we went to the clinic to pick her up, they advised us not to take her out, as she needed to stay there because the shelter did not have the proper equipment and she may become seriously dehydrated. I looked at my husband; our hearts were breaking for this poor little abandoned pup. We decided we would leave her there and ultimately be responsible for the vet bill.

When we arrived the next day, she looked much better and we decided to return her to the shelter. Ed and I knew we were getting attached to this sick little girl. We brought her back to the Humane Society where they put her in an isolation cage as she was contagious. Michelle told us we could visit her whenever we wanted. Consequently, we visited her daily for a week. Each day as she was getting stronger we were becoming more attached. One day Michelle told us they would be able to put her up for adoption soon. My heart sank! I was so drawn to this little girl, and I knew Ed was too. We went home and discussed what to do.

The next day we arrived at the shelter to pick up the new addition to our family. "Rusty" was a sweet, wild, crazy pup, who overcame many challenges. After surviving the life threatening parvo virus, Rusty developed an ongoing vaginal infection, then a dislocated knee cap, for which she needed surgery, and then mange, a skin condition that requires dips into a disinfecting solution once a week for six weeks. And this all occurred within the first year of her life. Ed and I began to believe she was invincible.

Throughout our years with Rusty, she became an irreplaceable member of our family. She knew our routines and could read our emotions by body language or tone of voice. She was a constant companion to both of us, but gravitated more to Ed. When Ed was diagnosed with terminal cancer, Rusty must have sensed it. She stayed by Ed's side as he became sicker and sicker from the chemo and radiation treatments. So much of our focus had been on Ed's illness that we overlooked a growing weakness in Rusty until, one day, she could not stand up. We rushed her to the vet to hear the unfortunate news that Rusty had cancer of the spleen and would likely die within weeks. The vet recommended we put her down, as she would suffer tremendously with this fast-growing cancer.

Ed and I discussed it, and we knew we did not want Rusty to suffer any longer. We told the vet our decision and he prepared a room so Ed and I could be with Rusty during her final moments. I could feel anxiety rising within myself as I had never been with anyone at the time of death. Throughout my childhood, my dogs just disappeared when they became ill or old.

We entered the room and Rusty was lying on a big pillow, looking very peaceful, and an IV was in her front leg. The vet told us when the injection would take place and when she would pass. Two small yelps and then Rusty was gone. Ed and I welled up with tears. As we looked at each other little did we know that this was Rusty's last gift to us. Six months later, as I held my husband's hand, I appreciated the gift Rusty had given me. In some small way Rusty had helped me to say good-bye to my husband and accept my unavoidable destiny.

Boots

I CAN'T BELIEVE IT'S been twenty years since I first saw those two little green eyes peering out at me through the bars of the cage. I tried to look away, but my eyes were locked and I knew I had been "picked." The paperwork was completed and the next day we picked up our six month old black and white kitten. Boots seemed the logical name since her tiny paws were all white. It didn't take long for Boots to put our sixty-three pound Collie Sheppard in her rightful place. I have had many cats throughout my life, but Boots was unique. She has never jumped on a countertop, ripped a curtain or clawed at the furniture. She was truly a dream come true.

Boots and I have shared many life events, as well as a home, longer than with anyone else in my entire life. She is an indoor cat who, fortunately, believes the only way to go outside is on a leash. At times I believe she actually thinks she is a dog. Boots has never been a lap cat, she is content to sit on her chosen perch and watch the world go by, in her own majestic way.

Through the years Boots and I have always had an unspoken respect for each other, while maintaining a courteous distance, but Boots and my husband Ed, were much more intimate. Every morning as Ed got ready for work Boots would join him in the bathroom and after twenty minutes they would both emerge bright eyed and ready to begin their day. I have to admit at times I was a bit jealous of their relationship.

When my grandchildren joined the family Boots knew to stay clear of flailing hands and wobbly feet. Boots travelled well in the car and also in the camper, which is a rarity for felines. By the time Boots was eight years old, she developed a cancerous tumour in one eye. The vet assured us it was not serious and is contained within the eye. Through the years Boots and I began to grow closer and occasionally she would lie beside me on the sofa. By the time she was ten years old, our lives had changed drastically as Ed had been diagnosed with terminal cancer. Boots seemed to sense his illness and began cuddling beside him in bed and on the sofa following a long day of chemotherapy treatments, while Rusty lay nearby on the floor. Our pets provided much needed comfort as we struggled through the trauma of our daily lives.

One day we noticed a weakness in Rusty's back legs and a trip to the vet revealed she had a deadly cancer, and would probably die within weeks; we chose to put her down. When we arrived home Boots was waiting for us, perched on the back of the sofa, looking as if she already knew Rusty wouldn't be coming home again. During the months ahead Boots was our ray of sunshine, always beside us providing warmth and tenderness to the very end of Ed's life. After Ed's passing Boots and I grew closer as we consoled each other during tear-filled days and nights.

Eventually the dreadful day came when I knew it was time to go through Ed's things. Through the blur of tear-filled eyes I gently folded Ed's clothing into piles. Initially Boots sat off to the side watching, then she sauntered over and began sniffing and rolling herself on top of the clothing. I knew this was her way of saying goodbye to a much loved friend. People say cats are aloof but I knew this wasn't true.

After much healing Boots and I moved on and developed a new life journey which now included Stan. Boots was happy to have another man in her life, as she readily snuggled up for chin rubs. When I began writing this story I feared it might have a different ending as Boots' health continues to decline having more bad than good days. Boots is a special cat and she and I will always share an exceptional part of each other's lives.

After-word: The story was supposed to end there, but since I first wrote this, Boots' health continued to deteriorate and, recently, she stopped eating. Sadly, I knew it was time to say goodbye to my loyal, faithful companion of twenty years. Boots peacefully closed her eyes and moved on to the journey that ultimately awaits us all. Till we meet again my dear sweet girl.

Family Letters
A Letter to My Brother

YOUR BIRTHDAY JUST passed and I thought about you, but then I think about you a lot. I remember when you would visit Grandma and Grandpa when I lived with them. You walked in with your wife and little son. You always dressed up for grandma, you looked so handsome. I was so proud to have you for my older brother. During the summer we would sit outside; you always with a beer in your hand. Grandpa loved to show you his latest creation—whether it was a sun room he was building or a new dog house for Sandy the boxer. Those were good times.

I can't remember my very young days with you, only through pictures. Thirteen years is a big age difference. You were an older brother to three sisters. We all adored you. That infectious laugh and down-to-earth way you had about you made it easy to be with you. Growing up in a dysfunctional family doesn't make it easy to stay connected, so we all drifted and found our own places in this world. You had your family and tried your best to keep them together, which seemed to result in a separation from your three sisters. I understood and I never held it against you. You were my brother and the love survived the years apart.

I remember reconnecting with your son and granddaughter and learning that you had cancer. I was determined to see you. When I walked in the hospital room, I only saw my handsome older brother with a big smile. I didn't see the hospital bed, the gown, or the tubes. The years melted away, the bond was still there. I sat at your bedside and we talked, a little awkward at first, but then easy and light. You were given two more years on this earth and we all came together for you. I could see that you were in pain, but you said you were fine, still being the big brother.

We talked about our families. I knew you felt bad for the years apart, but now you seemed to want to spend some time with your sisters. We didn't talk about the past, it wasn't important anymore. It was important that our hearts connected while there was still time. You never spoke about the end coming, but we knew it was soon. January 31, 2015, was the day we said goodbye. I will always miss you, but I will choose to remember our special time together rather than the years of distance, and be thankful that I had a wonderful big brother.

Dear Mom

ALTHOUGH YOU PASSED away many years ago, sometimes it seems like yesterday. Undeniably, you were not anywhere near the perfect mother, but I loved you and always felt loved by you. This may be difficult for some people to understand, as, for the most part, you didn't raise me. Being a single mother with four children was challenging back then, but not impossible, but this was not something you felt capable of undertaking.

I was the youngest of four, and the last to be sent away to live with friends of the family. It was a lonesome, isolating life for me and I lived for your visits. My excitement escalated as the day approached, but, more often than not, the visit would be cancelled at the last minute. I pretended to understand, but when I was alone in my room the tears flowed effortlessly. My heart ached, but I hid my tears because I feared Aunt Alice would say those hurtful words again. "See, she doesn't love you or she would have come to see you." I hated her words; I knew you loved me because I could feel it when we were together.

I struggled in my daily life, wishing I were home with you, as I didn't feel a part of this family. You promised we would be together someday and I clung to those words, hoping that day would be here soon. At school when others talked about their mothers my heart ached, I hoped no one would ask about my mom. I hesitated to tell them I was not with you, as I knew I would have to explain why and they would not understand. "Why don't you live with your mom? Who is that lady who picks you up?" I tried to avoid their questions. I told them Aunt Alice was my aunt, but she wasn't really, she was married to Mom's boyfriend's uncle. Aunt Alice was not a kind person, but maybe I felt that way because she wasn't you. She repeatedly criticized you and found fault with everything about you.

Finally you arrived to see me and looked so beautiful. Your arms enveloped me securely as I snuggled close and breathed in the smell of cigarettes and perfume. We often went for a drive and I sat close to you, while John sat on the other side. I loved to be close and touch you. At times we would go to a nearby park and you would carefully lay out a blanket on the grass for us to sit. We shared chocolate bars and orange pop, my favorite. Then you pulled your hairbrush out of your purse and began brushing my hair. "You look so beautiful sweetie," you would say. I thought to myself that I only felt beautiful when I was with you. I wished these days would last forever, but unfortunately they had to end and we both cried as we said goodbye. You always told me that soon we would all be together as a family. Your words gave me hope.

Sadly that day was a long time coming. I lived with you for only a brief time before I moved out on my own. By then I had become accustomed to being away from you and was proficient at hiding my pain and carrying on with life. In time, I got married. And soon after my own daughter was born. As I held her in my arms I knew I could never let her go. My love for her caused me to question how you could do what you did to your children. I became angry and didn't want to see you for a while. Eventually I needed to know how you could have given your children away. You cried and begged for my forgiveness. You said you thought your children would have a better life living with other people. I could see the pain in your eyes and I forgave you. We carried on from there, but things had changed and we only saw each other occasionally. As much as I say I forgave you, probably a little part of me was not able to forget the pain and longing in my heart.

When the call came that you had a heart attack, I was devastated. I could feel my breath catch as I raced to the hospital. You looked so fragile, but still my beautiful mother. I felt overwhelmed with love and faith you would not leave me again. You didn't speak, but I knew you were aware I was there beside you. They say the love between a mother and child never dies, and that was evident that day and every day since. You did rally. And stayed long enough for all of your children to visit and spend time with you. But my heart broke the day I had to say goodbye to you forever. I hope you and dad have found each other. Now it's my turn to say, one day we will all be together

Dear Dad

TODAY IS LABOR DAY and I can't help but remember you taking me to the Labor Day parade in Windsor. You always pushed me through the crowd to the front so I could see. I loved the marching band, as the pounding of the drums filled my chest with excitement. That was many years ago and one of my few memories of you. Unfortunately I never had the opportunity to really get to know you. Due to circumstances that I don't understand, you chose, for the most part, to be an absent parent. I don't know what happened between you and mom, and I don't want to judge, as I am aware that there are two sides to a story.

At eight years old I lived with you for one year. What I recall most was your great sense of humor – always joking with me and teasing. Friday was our special day. After you returned home from work we would jump on the bus and go downtown where you would buy me at least one storybook. One week it would be Cinderella, the next Pinocchio, leaving me with quite an enviable collection of books. This is how you fueled my lifelong love of books. During the year with you I missed Mom terribly, but I loved having my dad in my life. I learned quickly that you were not comfortable with displays of affection. Perhaps due to your English background? Whatever the reason, you rarely hugged me and only occasionally gave me a peck on the cheek.

That year passed quickly and I ended up back with mom. I don't remember the circumstances of my leaving you. Not even sure how my clothes and toys were transported to Mom's. Maybe it was a traumatic event, maybe you cried, and maybe I cried. I really don't know.

Through the years I infrequently visited you at your apartment. It was not a warm welcoming place, but I believe you tried to make me feel comfortable. You often had a bottle of beer nearby, but I don't recall you being intoxicated, or possibly I couldn't tell because I didn't know you that well. During our visits you sat on the chair and I on the sofa. The television played in the background to fill the silent pauses as you asked me all the superficial questions that you would ask someone you hardly knew. What's new? How is school? How is your sister? For which I often gave one-word answers. In spite of the awkwardness I looked forward to our visits because you were my dad. We were part of each other, as evident by our short big toe, wavy hair, and blue eyes. We never discussed Mom; I sensed you would have been uncomfortable if I were to mention her. I wasn't even sure if my siblings visited you, we never discussed it. Feelings and thoughts hung in the air like a heavy fog. We were not like a real family, just acquaintances.

When I got married you didn't attend my wedding, and I never asked why. But I didn't feel comfortable with anyone else giving me away, so I never walked down the aisle. We visited each other a few times after I was married, although the awkwardness prevailed. Unfortunately, there wasn't to be enough time for us to change this situation. Shortly after the birth of my daughter, you passed away, without ever having met her.

Your funeral was a surprisingly emotional experience for me, as the opportunity was gone to be any more than what we were to each other. I still miss you.

Love, your daughter.

Memorable People

Remembering a Less than Perfect Mother

This was written 20 years prior to the Dear Mom letter and the perceptions have remained the same.

May 10, 1979 feels like yesterday, yet it seems like a lifetime ago. I guess it's both. That was the day I said goodbye to my mother for the last time. I always refer to her as my mother, not Mom. I guess because she was more of a mother to me, than a mom. Mom's are there for you. They make you feel safe and cared for. Mothers are just that, your mother, a word, a title. I wished she had been more of a mom.

I WAS BORN LATE IN her life. By today's standards to have a baby at 34 isn't considered late, however, in the fifties women traditionally had their babies in their twenties. I was the fourth and youngest child. Perhaps she was tired of taking care of children by then, I don't know. Possibly being a woman alone with four children in the early 1950's was too hard for her. My memories are of always yearning for my mother to visit me, take me home, love me, accept me, and I guess maybe in her own way she did do some of those things, as much as she could anyway.

My visits with her were wonderful. I believe she tried to make up for all the lost time during those brief interludes. They say smell is one of the strongest triggers of memory. I suppose that's why I will always remember my mother's smell, a combination of perfume and cigarette smoke. During our visits she was very affectionate, hugging and kissing me. For those moments, I felt I belonged, she really did love me. "Can I come home to be with you?" I would ask, hoping maybe this time I would be able to be with her. "Soon dear, soon." She would say, as she attempted to distract me. "Do you want a manicure, how about if mom does your hair?" I always allowed her to do this, although the tears struggled to fill my eyes.

These brief visits ended far too quickly. We were both emotional when it came time to say goodbye. I never knew when I would see her again. Although she would tell me she would visit in a couple of weeks, I knew in my heart it would be longer. My heart ached as I watched her leave. It always took me a few hours to be able to talk to anyone after these visits. I just needed to be left alone.

As the years passed, my feelings of yearning changed to hurt and anger. I stopped waiting for her or believing that I would ever live with her again. Although I still looked forward to her visits, I pulled back a bit. I knew I had to protect myself from my mother. For some of my other siblings the pain was too much, they became angry and could not forgive. Therefore their relationship with her became simply one of visits on special occasions, like Christmas or birthdays.

When my daughter was born, my feelings for my mother changed, as I suppose would be normal. Your perception of everything changes when you become a parent. Your view of yourself, your family and your parents comes into question. As I held my tiny baby girl, I felt overwhelmed with emotion. How could my mother not feel those same feelings? Maybe she did and couldn't deal with them. Maybe she was aware of her own inadequacies and felt it would be better for me to be raised by other people who were better equipped to take care of me. I just wanted to be with her, but I didn't have a voice. I vowed never to allow my daughter to feel the pain I had felt. She would always have her mother with her; I would do everything to make her feel loved, secure and accepted.

My daughter was six years old when my mother died and she has only fleeting memories of her grandmother. She is now a grown woman with children of her own. Although at times we have had a difficult relationship, as most mothers and daughters do, I believe I did accomplish most of the tasks I set out to do as a parent. I still often think of my mother, and when I look back I think she did teach me an invaluable life lesson – how to be a good mom.

A Remarkable Woman

WHEN ASKED THE QUESTION, "Who is your most memorable person?" most people struggle to find an answer. But for me, it's easy. Irene Loraine Girard is the most memorable person in my life.

I first met Irene when I was sixteen years old and my social worker brought me to The Inn of Windsor. Bishop Carter of Windsor provided the seed money for Irene to fulfill her dream of opening a group home that would assist in equipping vulnerable young girls with the skills needed to survive on their own. After much searching, Irene found and purchased the perfect house, which she was able to turn into a home for girls aged 16 to 25 and she called it "The Inn." Because of my difficult family situation, my social worker, Carol, thought The Inn would be a possible solution, since it was a new group home for emotionally troubled girls. Carol made an appointment for us.

Irene was a gregarious woman of large stature with short, dark hair. She was cordial and welcoming to Carol and me and gave us a complete tour of this majestic, old home. She went over some of the rules and guidelines for living at The Inn. I was anxious to move in; I knew this was exactly where I wanted to be. I was the first girl to take up residence, although others rapidly followed. The Inn quickly filled up and Irene's dream was on its way to becoming a reality for hundreds of disadvantaged girls in the Windsor area.

The Inn became my home for the next year. I immediately loved Irene. Even though she was a bit stern, I found her caring and loving. Initially, Irene was spending almost twenty-four hours a day at The Inn and sleeping in her office. Occasionally she would have a volunteer come in and she'd be able to go home for the night. In time, she was able to secure funding to hire a full time housemother. This meant she was able to go home every night and even have the occasional weekend off, but she remained totally devoted to "her girls," and we all felt it. Not to say there wasn't conflict. When you have ten teenage girls there is undoubtedly going to be conflict. Irene handled this conflict well, with her calm and firm disposition. She had been raised in a loving, but strict, Catholic family, which ultimately provided her with many of the skills she needed to assist "her girls" at The Inn.

During my year at The Inn, Irene helped me to learn ways to overcome many childhood issues. She also supported me in obtaining employment, as I did not want to return to school. Eventually, I was able to move into my own apartment and support myself. The Inn supplied me with many of the household items I needed to set up my apartment. Even after moving out, Irene frequently invited me for a home-cooked meal. Throughout the next years I got married, moved away from Windsor, had a family, and, through it all, Irene continued to be a part of my life.

She never married. She felt The Inn was her calling in life and there was no room for anything or anyone else. When she retired, after twenty-five years at The Inn, I was invited to her retirement celebration as a special guest, and given a bursary to help pay for expenses, as I was completing my degree.

Irene often introduced me as her daughter and would introduce my daughter as her granddaughter. She was always there for me and I never felt it was a job for her, but rather that she genuinely cared about me and how I was doing in life. After her retirement, Irene continued to keep in touch with the girls at The Inn. Our visits often included Irene bringing me up to date on some of the latest situations there. A story she often repeated was when she was bitten on the arm by a girl in a fit of rage, whom she was trying to restrain. Often she would go into extensive detail about a particular girl, never revealing her name. I enjoyed hearing these stories as I shared her interest in psychology and social work.

But as time went on, I became more involved in my own life and we seemed to drift apart. I hadn't spoken to Irene for quite a while when I received a very disturbing letter from her. She had cancer. The letter assured me she was okay and not in any pain. I called her right away.

"Irene, I just got your letter. Are you okay?"

"Oh, yes, I shouldn't have told you in a letter, I should have called you, sorry Barb."

"What type of cancer do you have?"

"Multiple Myeloma." It is in my bones. I had a lot of pain but just thought it was my arthritis."

"Are you going to be okay?"

"I'm starting treatment next week."

"I'd like to come down and see you."

"Why don't you wait for a bit until we see how the treatment goes? I will let you know."

I waited for a couple of weeks, and then called again. Irene was home, and yes, I should come and visit. I was shocked when I saw her; she was no longer the strong, vibrant woman I knew. She was weak, frail, and had lost a ton of weight. I told her she looked good, as we often do when there is nothing else to say. We hugged, although she was apprehensive, as she explained her bones were very weak and painful. In fact, she told me she broke her shoulder while holding on to the counter to help get up from the toilet. I was unable to say anything; the words became lodged in my throat. As usual, Irene was able to read my face.

"That was a while ago, I'm better now, you are such a worrywart, Barb."

We said our goodbyes after a brief visit, and I promised to call her the next week. But, before I could, I received a call from Irene's niece. Irene was in the hospital, in a coma, with only days left. I told Paula I would be there soon. "No, Barb, she wouldn't know you were here, it's a long way to come. Irene knows how you feel about her. I will keep you updated." I reluctantly agreed to stay put. Two days later Irene was gone. I was heartbroken. The person who was always there for me and showed me how to overcome so much was now gone from this world.

I took time to grieve this special woman, but ultimately I knew Irene expected me to carry on and live the life that was given me.

The Inn of Windsor continues to fulfill Irene's dream and assist many young women to reach their potential and be all they can be.

Grandma

I STILL REMEMBER THE feeling when I came home to Grandma's house after an evening out with friends. The kitchen was softly lit with an under-the-counter fluorescent bulb, displaying a neat and orderly kitchen. I could hear the low murmur of the television in the next room and I knew Grandma and Grandpa were watching TV and, if it was a Sunday night, it would be *Bonanza*. I loved living here, I felt like I had finally found my forever home.

Grandma was small in stature, with white hair and smooth unlined skin. She suffered from a heart condition that prevented her from walking further than the house next door. Her back was curved with a Dowager's Hump that was so prevalent among older women at that time. My sister and I would jokingly tell her to straighten up and she would struggle to pull her shoulders back, but to no avail. As teenagers we just thought this is what happens to you when you get old. Grandma wore socks with sandals before it was fashionable. She also wore flowered housedresses and always an apron. Very little jewelry adorned her except her ring finger, upon which was a threadbare wedding band. She had not removed her ring for fifty-one years, as she believed that for each minute your ring was off your finger a tear would fall from your eye.

Grandma and mom did not get along and I did not understand why, as to me Grandma was a wonderful, loving, caring woman, whom I loved tremendously.

I went to live with my grandparents when I was fourteen years old. My life up to that point had been fraught with neglect, abuse, and abandonment, and the social system was running out of options as to where to put me. At this time Grandma was 70 years old and had always taken care of my uncle, who had some issues of his own. I wasn't sure whether grandma would take me in when she was approached by the social worker, but she did without hesitation.

Grandma had a warm, loving nature and she cared deeply for all her family members. She taught me what true devotion for your family really meant. As I settled into the routine of having normal meals, a cozy home, and not having to listen to drunken people fighting all the time, I felt a peace within myself. I knew this was what I wanted for my own life. Grandma not only cared for me, my sister, and my uncle, she also cared for Grandpa. His memory was failing and she did her best to fill in the time gaps and reassure him that everything was fine.

Saturday morning began as any other, as we all pitched in and did our chores, but something was different with Grandma. Several times I noticed her sitting on the sofa, obviously out of breath, anxiously twirling her fingers on the empty sofa cushion beside her. At one point I asked if she was alright, "Yes, Barb, I'm fine, just a little tired this morning." I was concerned, but then continued my cleaning. When we had finished our chores Grandma was warming up soup and making grilled cheese sandwiches for us. I just assumed she was fine as my sister and I chatted during our lunch. After lunch my sister went out with her boyfriend while I met friends nearby. In the back of my mind I thought about Grandma, but my thoughts were focused on my friends and having fun.

We all met at the neighborhood hang out and sat around drinking Coke and laughing. Out of the corner of my eye I saw my neighbor walk through the door and head in my direction. "Can you come outside for a moment Barb?" I followed her out. "I'm sorry to have to tell you this, but your grandmother has passed away and I think you should come home to be with your grandfather." I could feel my breath catch in my throat! It can't be, they must be mistaken! I sat silently in the car, feeling sick to my stomach and unable to talk.

As I walked through the door I saw Grandpa and Uncle Jack sitting at the kitchen table wiping tears away. Tears flooded my eyes as I hugged Grandpa and he whispered in my ear, "How can we go on without her?" It was the saddest day of my life. How would I go on without Grandma? Without the one who had saved me and given me my forever home? As in life, eventually we were all able to move on, even though an irreplaceable hole was left in our lives.

Inspiring Stories
Zac's Story

ZACHARY, MY GRANDSON, is a unique and special person. I know everyone thinks their grandchildren are special, but Zac (as he likes to be called) truly is, for many reasons.

Zac and his twin sister Madison were the first grandchildren born to both families. Within days of Zac's birth we were confronted with a devastating reality. Zac was born with a congenital heart defect called Truncus Arteriosus, a rare, heart problem that means there is only one large blood vessel leading out of the heart instead of the normal two. This usually comes with a hole between the two lower chambers of the heart, causing the oxygen-poor blood that is heading to the lungs to get mixed with the oxygen-rich blood coming from them and heading to the rest of the body. This causes severe circulatory problems that, if left untreated, can be fatal. (http://www.mayoclinic.org/diseases-conditions/truncus-arteriosus/basics/definition/con-20024974)

The difference between the two babies was striking. Madison was thriving while Zac struggled; even eating was hard for him. As I held Zac, trying to give him his bottle, his breathing was labored, and I could see his chest contracting under his ribs as he gasped for air. It was so disturbing that

I mentioned it to his ICU nurse. We all tried in vain to encourage Zac to take his bottle, but he was just too tired and weak to suck. Ultimately, a feeding tube was inserted. As Zac continued to fade, we were told he needed lifesaving surgery as soon as possible. At thirteen days old Zac was scheduled for open-heart surgery. He would be kept alive by way of a heart-lung machine during the six-hour operation. My daughter and her husband were told he would not live longer than a few months without the surgery. It was a distressing reality as we were torn between happiness when we were with Madison and sadness when we were with Zac.

Zac's ICU nurse suggested we have him baptized prior to the surgery. So mom and dad decided they would have the babies baptized together. Godparents were chosen and a priest was called in. It was heart-breaking to witness these two newborns lying together in the incubator. Two beautiful babies, dressed in nighties and frilly bonnets for their baptism. One expressing a loud, robust voice with arms and legs flailing, while the other lay still, pale and lifeless. Zac was on medication to keep him as still as possible and preserve his strength for the upcoming surgery.

Days later, the families gathered in a small room, waiting for the outcome of the long, painstaking surgery. Madison was with us and provided a much-needed distraction. There was an overwhelming sense of relief when we were finally told the surgery was a success. One month later, Zac was back home with his sister. Tears welled in my eyes as Zac lay in the crib beside his sister. His cry was that of a sick baby. He was so thin and weak and his head had been shaved on one side for the IV. It really was a heartbreaking site and I couldn't prevent my tears from falling on his little blanket. The healing process was long and heart-rending, with everyone pitching in to help the parents. In the meantime, we all fell in love with these two little warriors.

Everything seemed to be going well until Zac was six months old. He began to struggle with his breathing again. During his appointment with the cardiologist it was discovered that his pulmonary arteries were not growing, and he was going to have to undergo another procedure. The surgeon assured us this would not be nearly as invasive as the initial procedure: he would go through the groin to insert the two stents needed to open up Zac's pulmonary arteries. We steeled ourselves as best we could for the surgery. I took care of Madison, and the other grandparents travelled with mom and dad to the Toronto Sick Kids Hospital. Within a few days Zac was home and on the mend. He was a little cranky, but still a lovable boy. A baby swing proved to be a lifesaver, providing Zac a distraction from his pain, and a needed break for those caring for him.

Zac got over this hurdle and began to thrive. His engaging personality was undeniable; he was a totally unselfish and loving boy who readily shared with his sister. Through the next few years Zac was closely monitored by a cardiologist, and, eventually, he began school with his sister. There were no obvious signs of the trauma Zac had experienced so far in his brief life, with the exception of the scar on his chest. At five years old he began to play hockey and loved it. One year he even made the competitive team. I had always been doubtful that Zac would be able to play hockey - fortunately, I was wrong. Although a good player, he lacked endurance on the ice. He often returned to the bench, sick to his stomach. But that didn't prevent him from going right back out on the ice. It pulled at my heartstrings to see the little trouper he was as he skated with his friends trying so hard to keep up.

The years passed and Zac developed into a wonderful boy and teenager. Eventually he would need more surgery, but nobody knew when that would happen. Every check-up was filled with anxiety until his parents were able to reassure us that he was fine. But then the day arrived. Zac was almost fifteen and completing his first year of high school when the cardiologist told him that the time had come for his surgery. He bravely asked the cardiologist only one question: afterward, would he finally be able to keep up with the other kids? The cardiologist was tactful in telling Zac that he would feel much better and have more energy, but was careful not to make false promises. The brave front fell when Zac was alone with his mom. Then the tears came. But only briefly. Zac would face this surgery as he faced everything in his life, courageous and strong.

The surgery was to replace the donor valve that had been inserted when he was thirteen days old, plus his stents would be expanded to accommodate his growing body. We had always been told he would have to have open-heart surgery to change the valve, but, with medical advances, they were able to do both procedures through the groin. This would help to speed the recovery, and it was so fast that only a little more than a week after surgery he was able to try out for the badminton team and he made it! I felt my breath catch as I was overcome with pride, but I didn't want to make too much of a fuss.

The surgery had given him increased blood flow that allowed his heart to function more efficiently, providing him with much needed energy and increased endurance. I suggested he try out for hockey again, but by now he was spending most of this free time working at a job he enjoyed and had lost interest in hockey. His sister, Madison, has since picked up the hockey torch and become an awesome goalie.

Zac is now sixteen years old and doing all the typical things teenagers do. He is good looking, popular, well liked, and seems to be able to take most things in stride. A memorable day occurred recently when Zac asked me if he could have twenty dollars to go to the movies with his friends. I had already planned to give him forty dollars, as I had bought his sister some clothes. But when I gave Zac the forty dollars, he handed me back a twenty-dollar bill and said "I don't need this grandma." Anyone who has teenagers will understand how truly remarkable this was. As I looked into his eyes I felt a tug at my own heart, because I knew there was nothing wrong with his, and he was a truly special human being. Zac will probably need more procedures throughout his life, but, with his attitude, I know he's capable of handling those ups and downs. After all, he's a survivor.

Love After Loss

THE DEATH OF MY HUSBAND, following a brief fight with cancer, left me totally devastated. The overwhelming grief was extremely difficult to go through, but I knew I had no choice. To cope, I thought it might help if I fulfilled some of the dreams Ed and I had together. We had often discussed taking our grandchildren to Disney World in Florida, and I felt it might be a healing trip for us. After booking the trip, my next priority was finding someone to watch Suzie. Suzie is a little black and white Bichon/Poodle I had found on Kijiji a few weeks before Ed's death. He had encouraged me to get a puppy to keep me company after his passing. Fortunately, my neighbor, who had watched Suzie while I was staying in the hospital with Ed during his final days, was more than willing to watch her while we were in Florida.

The trip was difficult, filled with tears and sadness, but also some good times. I was happy to get home, and immediately went to Eleanor's to pick up Suzie. While there, Eleanor mentioned that the man on the corner had lost his wife a few days ago, and that maybe I could talk to him. I didn't recall ever seeing the man she mentioned. She went on to describe him to me and told me that he walks a little black dog. I never gave it much thought until a few days later.

I was out in my garage when I saw the man walking a little black dog. I walked up to him and asked him if he had just lost his wife. I don't know what made me approach him, it was so unlike me, but it felt like the right thing to do. He confirmed he had, and I could see the sadness in his face, and I knew how he felt. I told him I had just lost my husband as well. He looked down, obviously not sure what to say. So I assured him things would get better and he went on his way.

During the course of the next year I saw Stan, four or five times. Each time we talked briefly about missing our loved ones. Since I was ahead of him in the grieving process I always assured him things would get better. He was very quiet but pleasant. I felt drawn to him, but I thought it was due to our mutual loss.

It had been over a year, but my grief was still all consuming. I knew I needed to get involved in something, so I decided to take golfing lessons. One day while I was putting my clubs in the trunk and getting ready to go to my last lesson, Stan came walking by with his dog, Joey.

"How you doing?" he said casually.

"Going to my last golf lesson."

"You golf?"

"Well, not sure if I would say that, but I'm learning."

"We should go golfing sometime."

"Sure!"

"Okay I think I have your number, I'll give you a call next week."

I wasn't sure if I really wanted to go with him, but then I thought, "Well, It's only a game of golf." A few days later he called and we went golfing. I had so much fun, I briefly forgot my grief. However, the next few days were filled with confusion and guilt. How could I go out and have fun with another man! Stan called again and I reluctantly went to dinner and a movie. Ultimately we began seeing each other on a regular basis. I struggled terribly with the guilt, but Stan seemed to be handling things well. At times I pushed him away; only to draw him close again later. We both persevered, as there seemed to be an attraction between us that was difficult to ignore.

As we got to know each other we agreed the parallels in our situations seemed to be more than coincidence. We had both lived in the same unit within our condo complex, where some units are similar, but not exactly the same. This would not be that significant on its own, but when you add all the incidents together the parallels are quite unique. Stan moved into the complex six months after Ed and me. We had both viewed many homes before settling on this one. My husband passed away two and a half years after moving in and Stan's wife also passed away after living in the condo for two and a half years. We had both been attending the same Cancer Unit for treatments, but never seemed to run into each other. Then there was the fact that Eleanor had been Stan's neighbor and mentioned him to me. I call her our angel on earth. It does seem that there were a few hands arranging for us to meet. Ultimately, we found our way through the grief, the loss, and discovered a special love. A love we both never would have thought possible. Two years ago, we married. We now share a deep understanding and a bond that I know will carry us through till death do us part.

Love Beyond Tragedy

ON SEPTEMBER 15, 2018 we attended the wedding of Jenn, my brother's granddaughter. A few years earlier my sisters and I had been reunited with my brother Lyle and his family, following a long estrangement. When Lyle became ill, we were grateful to Jenn for contacting us and giving us the opportunity to spend some time with Lyle and heal old wounds before his passing. When we heard of Jenn's wedding, I wasn't sure we would be invited because of the years of estrangement. We knew the wedding day would be bitter sweet because of the tragedies that had occurred in Jenn's family in the previous few years.

The wedding was beautiful, even though so many people who should have been there were no longer with us. In 2014, shortly after we were reconciled with the family, Jenn's mother, Janet, was killed in a lone vehicle accident while delivering newspapers during the early morning hours. Reports say she fell asleep at the wheel and was killed instantly. My sisters and I did not know the family well, but couldn't help but feel the pain and loss they were experiencing.

Janet was a beautiful and devoted wife, young mother and grandmother, who had just turned 47 years old. The loss of Janet was unbearable to her family—her husband, Mike, daughter Jenn, and son Josh, plus four young grandchildren.

The family pulled together and supported each other through anguished tears. At the time, Jenn's three children and Josh's young daughter, Aaliyah, were unable to grasp the magnitude of the loss of their grandmother. When I saw the family, I had no idea what to say to them—how do you get over such a shock. Josh was in his twenties, still living at home with his father, and Aaliyah was often with him so they were a comfort to Mike. My brother, Lyle, who was in hospital and nearing the end of his life, was devastated by the loss of Janet. We tried to offer the family as much support as we could under the circumstances.

Our time with my brother was short. On January 31, 2015, just three short months after Janet passed, Lyle took his last breath. My heart ached for all the lost time we would never recover. This was another blow to the family—still raw from the death of their beloved Janet.

Following the death of my brother, we kept in contact with the family. My sisters and I wanted to be a part of their lives and even went on a family camping trip with them, as they were learning to live with their new normal.

Josh met a great girl and they found a house and moved in together. Always the adventurous type, Josh decided to buy a motorcycle. He was beginning to enjoy life again and often out riding with his buddies. Then the unthinkable happened. On his way to work one morning he was involved in a collision. He received massive head injuries and was rushed to the hospital. Jenn and Mike and a group of Josh's closest friends gathered together in the hospital waiting room sharing stories of Josh, all hopeful he would recover. When Mike and Jenn were called into a private room with the doctor, they both knew it wasn't going to be good. The doctor informed them that Josh had no chance of surviving and that it would be best to remove him from life support. The pain was too familiar, less than two years after the death of Josh's mother and grandfather, another loss. Life support was removed on July 19, 2016 and the family had to say a tearful good bye to a young son, brother, and father. Not wanting to intrude on their grief, my sisters and I kept a distance but offered support when possible.

Jenn carried on her daily life, while unable to ignore the tremendous loss of her mother and brother. She cared for her three children, supported her dad and maintained a special relationship with Josh's daughter Aaliyah. Eventually I became aware from Facebook posts that there was a new man in Jenn's life. Chad and Jenn seemed to be a good fit and we were happy there was finally some happiness in the family. We believed the losses were over, until we were all on a camping trip and I received a call that my older sister was in the hospital with pneumonia. One year after Josh's passing my sister passed. More pain, more loss, four deaths within four short years. Our hearts were heavy with tears, but choices are limited, we have to go on.

September 15, 2018, was a wedding day that provided renewed hope for everyone. Jenn and her new husband Chad had found each other. Chad had been fighting his own demons and Jenn was able to rise up from the pain and loss in her own life to help Chad begin again. The wedding was beautiful. All the people who had been lost in the years before were clearly represented at this wedding. When Josh's young daughter walked down the aisle with Jenn's daughter, I felt the tears well up, as I'm sure most people did. I believe Chad and Jenn were brought together to heal each other and create a beautiful life together.

No matter what life dishes out, we all have to make choices for our future.

Life Changing
A Memorable Day

I LIFTED MY HEAD; THE silence was deafening, interrupted only by the sound of Mary moaning from somewhere behind me. Everything was dark and cold, and all I could smell was gasoline. I pulled myself out through the windshield of the car and went to the driver's side. Rick was lying still and I could see a blanket on his head. I pulled the blanket off, but he didn't move. I started to cry; I was frightened and was having a hard time standing. I screamed for my sister, and then blacked out.

The next sounds I heard were sirens growing louder and louder. There was a lot of commotion and I heard one of the attendants say "It's too late for this one." I felt my body tighten, oh no, not Mary! Someone lifted me onto a stretcher and I asked about my sister.

"Was she in the back seat?"

"Yes."

"We're getting her out now." I felt relieved. As the ambulance was driving to Leamington General Hospital, I asked the attendant sitting with me how everyone else was, and that's when he told me that the driver didn't make it, but that the other fellow in the back was okay. I could feel my breath catch in my throat and the tears stream out of my eyes. The tightness in my chest was so painful that I tried to grab myself, but I wasn't able to move my arms.

Jan was lying on the stretcher beside me in the emergency department. The blood was soaking through the wrapping on her arm. I knew she could hear what I was hearing – the disturbing moaning from my sister. Tears were running out of her eyes. "Did they tell you about Rick?" I nodded. It was all surreal. Was this a dream? It couldn't be real. My mind searched to make some sense of what was happening. I had gotten on the bus that morning to go to school, just like any other morning; how did I end up here?

I couldn't believe Rick was dead, this was our first date!

Jan was wheeled away to another room, and then I saw Gary being pushed by in a wheelchair. My leg began to feel strange, like it was being squeezed and my head ached. Dried blood was on my hands. I saw a gash on my thumb, but I wasn't sure where all the blood was coming from. That's all I remember until the next day.

A nurse gently woke me up. I didn't say anything; I was waiting for her to tell me what had really happened. She reaffirmed the words I had heard the night before. Rick was dead; my sister was critically injured and in a coma. My head began to hurt, I felt sick to my stomach and dizzy, so the nurse gave me something for the pain and I went to another surreal place until mom and my older sister arrived. They took me to see Mary. She was still moaning, but not as loudly. Her head was bandaged and when she moved I could see the dried blood that had come through onto the pillow. Her eyes were open a bit and looked almost black. The doctor said she was in a coma. Again I could hardly breathe as the tears welled in my eyes. Later that day someone brought in a copy of *The Windsor Star*. On the front page was the caption *What's Left of Death Car* and below was a picture of Rick's mangled car. As I lay in the hospital bed, my mind struggled to remember the events before the accident. I remembered Rick drinking beer and throwing the empty bottles out the window. We were all laughing, as he was swerving the car through the winding roads of Point Pelee National Park. We were young and invincible, or so we thought. It was a time when drinking and driving was not talked about. Someone challenged Rick to go faster and that's the last thing I remember, until waking up in the car.

The next morning when the doctor came in on his rounds he said something to me that would affect the rest of my life. "Well Barbara, God must have had his arms around you protecting you, since the accident happened all around you." At the time they were just words, but as my life went on, I began to believe that maybe there was a reason why I was put on this earth and living this life.

Myself, Jan, and Gary, were released from the hospital a week later but the emotional and physical recovery has been a long process. My sister suffered many broken bones and remained in a coma for weeks. She still continues to suffer the effects of a traumatic brain injury. Its sad how one single event can have such a devastating and lasting impact on so many lives.

A Life Altering Day

My sister, Mary, and I were incarcerated in Ontario Training Schools for Girls, at 12 and 13 years old. Training schools are better known as reform schools. At that time, all I knew about reform school was what I had seen in movies and on television shows. Reform schools were portrayed as places where girls and boys are sent to be punished for bad behaviour. The truant officer had warned us that this is where we would end up if we didn't go to school, but we never believed it would actually happen. I thought people got sent to training school only if they had committed a crime. I didn't realize that not going to school was a crime. Our parents were mostly concerned with meeting their own needs, so my sister and I were left to our own devices, and, as you can imagine, attending school wasn't part of our agenda.

FOLLOWING MY PARENTS' unemotional testimony in Family Court, Mary and I hugged them both and said a tearful goodbye. We were taken away by a court official to a waiting car containing two middle-aged men. My stomach began to tighten as I tried to convince the men to stop by our house so we could grab a few things. My plan was to escape, but one of the men said that wasn't possible and we were abruptly on our way to Galt Reception Center, in the community of

Cambridge, Ontario. We were scared—unaware of what was ahead for us. For the most part, the men ignored us while chit chatting with each other throughout the long drive.

My experience in Galt Training School and, later, Kawartha Lakes School in Lindsay, Ontario, was one of the worst experiences of my life. The atmosphere in the Training School was oppressive, controlling, and regimented. It seemed the intention was to steal our identity—to remake us into the type of people they felt we should be. We were treated like criminals; so I began to believe I really must be a bad person. Over time, I became withdrawn and rarely spoke to anyone, and, since my sister and I were separated, I felt extremely alone.

The school was organized on a point system, points for housekeeping, grooming, and good behaviour. At the end of the week the four girls with the most points would receive a ribbon. Bullying was a normal part of life in training school. Punishment was harsh. If you broke a rule your punishment would be to lose one of the few privileges you had, or having to scrub the gym floor on hands and knees, or the ultimate punishment: being sent to solitary confinement, better known as The Hole. There was no privacy in training school. All our personal activities were scrutinized closely by the staff, even having a shower. It was a humiliating experience to say the least. All I wanted to do was get out of there. Training School turned me into a totally submissive person; I became the person they wanted me to be. If that was the only way to get out, that's what I would do. However, in the process of becoming who they wanted me to be, I lost my self.

After six months I was released to a foster home. The foster home was a further continuation of abuse. I became a broken person, with no self esteem and little hope of finding any happiness in this life, but I continued to search. I looked for happiness in an early marriage, the birth of my daughter, re-educating myself, but nothing brought me that systemic feeling of happiness. I believed I had to keep my shameful secret and never let anyone know I had been sent to that place where bad boys and girls go to get fixed.

One day, while I was watching a Canadian news program, W5, everything changed. The commentator began talking about Ontario Training Schools and how children had been unfairly incarcerated and treated like criminals. My eyes and ears were glued to the TV. The reporter was interviewing a man who had been sent to Training School as a young boy. He talked about the shame he felt, the low self esteem, that feeling of being intrinsically bad. The same feelings I felt and had kept buried all these years. At the end of the program, a link was shared where more information could be found about an ongoing Class Action Suit[1] for Crown Wards who had been incarcerated between certain years. I immediately went on the site and found more information. I filled out the application and, through tear filled eyes, revealed my story in detail for the first time.

Within a week I was contacted and told I was included in the Class Action Suit and I was advised to apply to The Criminal Injuries Board for compensation. I filled out the extensive application for the Criminal Injuries Board and was granted the maximum award. It was not a lot of money, but,

---

1.   https://kmlaw.ca/cases/ontario-training-schools/

for me, it was validation that I had been treated unfairly. I felt as if I was finally able to breathe in a way that I hadn't since I was 12 years old, before this nightmare had taken over my life. I was not a bad person; the people who did this to me were the bad people. I felt the rebirth of the 12-year-old girl I had lost so many years ago. Everything looked different, everything felt different; I now looked through the eyes of a woman who was in the process of being healed from a terrible wrongdoing.

My hope is that telling my story would be beneficial to other women who have been sent to Training School, so they will be able to share their truth and realize this was not their fault and finally begin to live their life.

The class action suit is expected to go to trial in 2021, and, with a positive outcome, thousands of girls and boys will be vindicated and finally be able to live the rest of their lives with the knowledge that they were not the bad children that the Province of Ontario had convinced them they were so many years ago.

Part 2

Short Fiction and Poetry

Ashley Mae's Dark Day

ASHLEY MAE SAT QUIETLY in the living room watching *Caillou* on television as she did most Sundays. It was her favorite show, but today felt different than most Sundays. Something was wrong with her parents. During breakfast they didn't talk to each other, but they did to Ashley Mae. Their smiles were not like real smiles, but more like the smiles Ashley painted on her pictures at school. She wondered why her parents were mad at each other.

Ashley wished Caillou's voice were louder so it would drown out the angry voices now escaping from the kitchen. She grabbed Betsy close to her.

"It's okay, they'll stop soon, don't cry Betsy." Ashley Mae wanted to be strong for Betsy. Betsy had been with her since she could remember. Her mother told her that Aunt Carol had given Betsy to her as a Christmas gift. The voices grew heavier, angrier. Caillou's small voice almost unheard now. Ashley wondered how it would end this time. Would she go to her grandma's house, or maybe Aunt Carol's? She liked to go to Grandma's, it was quiet there; she could play with Betsy and even watch television and hear all the words.

"Fine I'm leaving, but this time I'm never coming back!" Ashley was scared, but she was more worried about Betsy. She held her closer as her mother rushed into the room.

"Come on baby, we're leaving." Ashley didn't want to leave her dad, but she didn't want to make her mom mad. She glanced briefly at her father as she grabbed Betsy and rushed to keep up with her mother. As they jumped in the car her mother jerked it into reverse and they raced out the driveway. Ashley wondered where they were going. Her mother was driving in silence, but Ashley could tell she was angry, very angry. Her mother's mouth was stiff like it was when Ashley did something her mother disapproved of. She didn't recognize any of the streets or houses they were driving by.

"Where are we going Mommy?"

"Don't worry baby, we're going to a safer place."

Ashley wondered what she meant; maybe they were going to Grandma's house, but she knew this wasn't the way to Grandmas. They pulled up to a house Ashley had never seen before. Her mother knocked on the door very quickly and loudly. Ashley still held Betsy close, as a man opened the door.

"Can I come in?" Her mother's voice sounded relieved to find this man at home, yet tears flowed down her face.

"Sure, what's wrong?"

"He knows about us."

Ashley wondered what she was talking about. She had never seen this man before, but her mother seemed to know him well.

"This is Ashley." Her mother said hurriedly without telling Ashley the man's name. The man nodded his head briefly in Ashley's direction and turned back to her mother. He put his arms around her mother and held her as she cried. Ashley wondered what he was doing with her mother. She had only seen her dad or Uncle Kevin touch her mother in this way. The man turned on the television for Ashley. He seemed to want to keep Ashley away from them. Again she sat watching and listening to Caillou. This time she could hear all the words, but her mind was thinking of her dad. She wondered if he had ever been in this man's house. Her mind shifted to Caillou. What would Caillou do if he were in this house? Caillou was six years old just like Ashley Mae, but he would probably know what to do.

Her mother and the man had been talking in the kitchen for a long time, but their voices were low, so she didn't know what they were saying. Suddenly Ashley felt hungry, she realized they hadn't eaten any lunch and it was almost suppertime. She knew it was dinner time because her belly hurt and because *Dora the Explorer*, her second favorite show was almost over. Her mother began shuffling dishes around in the kitchen. Ashley felt different at this man's house, not comfortable like she did at home or at grandma's house. She just sat on the couch with Betsy, wishing her mother would come and sit with her, but she didn't. Her mother just kept talking to the man whose house they were in. The pain in Ashley's belly seemed to get worse. She felt like she wanted to throw up, but swallowed hard. Ashley didn't want anyone to get mad at her, so she just sat and waited, swallowing hard to contain the sickness in her stomach.

A different show came on the television; it had puppets singing happy songs. Ashley thought this show was too young for her, but she didn't want to ask her mom or the man to change it, so she just sat, clinging to Betsy. She heard a loud bang on the door. Her mother and the man stopped talking. Ashley thought they were answering the door. She called to her mother.

"Shhh!" Her mother said as she looked into the living room where Ashley Mae was sitting. Ashley didn't know why everyone was so quiet. Who was at the door? The knocking got louder. Ashley could tell her mother was afraid, therefore she became afraid. She started chewing on Betsy's arm, not sure if she would be able to stop herself from throwing up. The banging got louder and louder.

"I know you're in there, open up, I want to see my daughter!"

Ashley wanted to go to her dad, but fear paralyzed her. No one said a word. The only sound was the banging on the door. Ashley thought the door was going to fall into the kitchen. She wanted to cry, but felt numb with fear.

After a loud thump, the door fell to the kitchen floor. Ashley ran behind the couch and hid. The next sound she heard was a loud bang; it was so loud it hurt Ashley's ears. Then her mother screamed, but only briefly, then another loud bang. Ashley no longer heard her mother's voice. She grabbed Betsy and stood up for a moment but couldn't see her mom or the man, only her dad stood looking down; his face looked funny, not like it usually did.

"Daddy!" She tried to run toward her father but couldn't. A sharp pain pierced her chest as she dropped to the floor, before being engulfed by the bright light.

Mysterious Pursuer

ELLEN STOOD ANXIOUSLY at the bus stop, her eyes darting nervously back and forth. She searched the streets for the shiny black car with the tinted windows. Not wanting to draw attention to herself, she attempted to move with ease. Panic shook her body, as she stepped nearer to the curb and gazed down the street hoping to see the bus. Instead she saw it. The black car parked a short distance down the street, the circular headlights glaring like arrows piercing her soul. Ellen wanted to scream. She tried to calm herself. Please Lord make the bus come soon – Ellen prayed silently to herself.

Within seconds the bus arrived. Ellen walked straight to the back of the crowded bus. Tired, drawn faces encircled her. She couldn't help but look out the back window. There it was, the third car behind the bus, she swallowed hard and turned away.

The force of the bus stopping propelled Ellen forward causing her to bump into the lady with the red blazer, who abruptly gathered her bags and pushed her way toward the open door. Ellen dropped into the still warm seat. Staring straight ahead she fought the urge to look back. She knew the car would still be following. For almost two weeks now she had been pursued by this same mysterious vehicle. Ellen took a deep breath as her apartment building came into view. She reached up and pulled the cord for her stop. Without looking around she hurried to the entrance. Once inside her apartment she hooked the chain and double locked the door, feeling safe within her own four walls. As she quickly drew the blinds, a bright glare caught her eye. There it was on the street below- the sun shining off the chrome mirror on the driver's side.

"Why me! Why! What does this person want from me?" Ellen cried out in frustration.

That night, as in every night for the past two weeks, Ellen's sleep was plagued with terrible visions of being kidnapped, beaten, even killed. Just before her demise she would wake up, her nightgown drenched in perspiration. In the morning she rushed to the window, hoping the whole thing had been a bad dream. There it was, the eerie sight of the lone black car waiting like a vulture. Who was inside? The smoky windows prevented her from seeing. Feeling helpless Ellen searched her soul for any clue as to who might want to do this to her. Was it any of her friends, ex-friends, boyfriends, ex-boyfriends? The answer was always the same unremitting no. Ellen had very few friends; her focus has always been her career, as she was often accused of being a workaholic.

Ellen wanted to tell her parents, but knew she couldn't. They were getting on in years and their health had been failing recently. Jennifer was the only person who knew.

"Ellen you've got to report this to the police." Jennifer's words were insistent.

"I don't want to make a big deal about it."

"Come on Ellen. There's obviously some weirdo in that car. Who knows what he'll do next."

Ellen thought about what Jennifer had said. She knew she was right. The next morning she called the police department and made an appointment to meet with an officer at her apartment. That evening a gentle rapping disturbed Ellen's tormented thoughts.

"Who is it?"

"It's Officers Brennan and McGee."

Ellen looked through the peep hole. There stood two middle age men.

"How do I know you're police officers?"

Suddenly her view of the officers was disturbed, by a silver badge accompanied by a picture of the man who was speaking. She opened the door.

"Miss Jackson?"

"Yes."

"I'm Officer Brennan and this is Officer McGee." He couldn't help but notice a subtle beauty about Ellen as she smiled slightly. She shook each of their outstretched hands.

"Sorry about the uniforms. We felt due to the nature of the situation it would be best if we came in plain clothes. We didn't want to draw any undue attention to ourselves."

Officer Brennan asked questions while Officer McGee took notes. As Ellen told her story, she felt somewhat relieved to be finally disclosing it.

"Is the car outside right now?"

"Yes I believe so."

"Would you mind going to the window to see if you can identify it for us?"

Ellen apprehensively went to the window.

"Yes it's there. It's right across the street."

"Okay on our way out we'll get the license plate number. You did you say you weren't able to obtain the number did you not?"

"No I'm sorry, I never even thought of it."

"That's okay. You get a good night sleep Miss Jackson." Ellen smiled, feeling somewhat safer now.

"We'll let you know if we learn anything about this guy." Officer Brennan closed the door as he left. Ellen immediately locked the door, then finished her dinner and went to bed.

After another agonizing night's sleep Ellen awoke with a throbbing headache. There was no way she could go to work. She looked out the window and there it was, like a vulture it stood, nameless, faceless, waiting for its prey. After calling work Ellen tried to rest, but was startled by the ringing of her phone.

"Hello."

"Hello Miss Jackson." Ellen recognized the voice.

"Oh hello Officer Brennan. Have you got any news for me?" She asked apprehensively.

"Well actually yes. The car belongs to a David Miles; he lives at 108 Glengarry here in town."

"David Miles?" Ellen questioned.

"Does that name mean anything to you?"

"No, nothing. I don't know anyone by that name. What does he want with me?"

"We are hoping to find that out when we talk to him. We'll be going over to his house later this evening. Try to stay indoors until we find out what David Miles has on his mind."

Ellen agreed. She looked out the window. There it was. She hated that car, she wanted to rush down there and scream – LEAVE ME ALONE! Somehow she felt even more frightened knowing the name of the person inside.

Who was David Miles and what did he want with her? Ellen spent the day in her apartment pacing nervously to and from the window. It was almost 10 o'clock when she went to bed enduring another restless night. As soon as she got up in the morning she looked out the window and was startled to see the car was nowhere in sight. Perhaps the police had scared him off. In that instant the phone rang.

"Hello."

"Good morning Miss Jackson, Officer Brennan here. Officer McGee and I would like to escort you to work this morning. What time do you usually leave?"

"Around 8:30. Why? What's happened?"

"Oh there's nothing to worry about. This is just a precautionary measure."

"Did you talk to this David Miles? What does he want from me?"

"Yes we did but now is not the time to talk. We'll discuss it with you later."

When they arrived Officer Brennan avoided answering Ellen's multiple questions.

"Now we want you to go to work the same way you do every day. Use the same route." Officer McGee said as they followed Ellen toward the elevator. She pressed B for basement. As soon as the elevator door opened to the parking garage the officers instantly moved in front of Ellen, almost like a shield. Within seconds she felt herself being pushed, then heard a deafening bang. Officer Brennan was enveloping Ellen behind a cement pole. Officer McGee was perched, gun in hand, behind another pole. Ellen was frozen in fear. Seconds later she heard the roar of a car. Then she heard a barrage of gunshots and a loud crash. Ellen buried her face in Officer Brennan's chest. The only sound left was that of a car horn screaming.

Officer Brennan pulled away. Ellen looked up. Her eyes resting on a haunting sight. The shiny black car was wrapped around a pole. The dark windows were all but gone. Fragments of glass still framed a jagged windshield; inside she could see a blood stained man's face, his body lying lifeless across the steering wheel. The horn was deafening. Office McGee gently pushed the body back from the steering wheel.

Ellen searched the face. Nothing was familiar. She was overcome with anguish. Why did this horrible thing happen to her? She turned questioningly to Officer Brennan.

"David Miles was a troubled man. That became painfully apparent from our conversation with him yesterday."

Ellen didn't know what to say. Without them she feared she would have been dead. She couldn't believe how quickly it was over. Weeks and weeks of torment over in a matter of seconds.

Ellen stayed home from work for the next few days. Jennifer came over to check on her.

"Ellen aren't you at all curious why this maniac was after you?"

"Yes."

"Then call the Police Department and insist on some answers."

"I guess I should."

The next morning Ellen called Officer Brennan. He came over that evening.

"Were you able to find out why David Miles was after me?"

"Yes, we think we know." Officer Brennan knew Ellen deserved some answers. He reached into his inside jacket pocket.

"Here, have a look at this." He handed her a snapshot. Ellen felt as though someone had knocked the wind out of her. The woman in the picture was almost a mirror image of herself.

She searched the face, the eyes – the only difference was that the woman in the picture had longer hair than Ellen:

"Who is this woman?" Ellen asked when she was able to regain her composure.

"This is a picture of David Miles' estranged wife Judy. She could be your twin."

"Oh my God, he must have thought I was her!" Ellen gasped.

"Well the story goes that Judy Miles took their three children and disappeared. Prior to her disappearance, Judy Miles charged her husband with assault. Apparently this wasn't the first time she had called the police. David Miles was not a stable person. His wife leaving just seemed to push him over the edge."

Ellen listened intently as Officer Brennan continued.

"Apparently after she left, David had a complete breakdown and has been in and out of psychiatric hospitals since. Many people had overheard him say he would kill his wife if he ever found her."

"So he thought I was his wife."

"Seems that way."

A few days later Ellen decided she needed to see her parents. She put her suitcase in the trunk and headed up north. She was trying to imagine how her parents would react when she told them what had happened. Her parents had always been very open about the fact that she had been adopted. However, up until now Ellen had never had an interest in finding her biological parents. Her life had been secure and happy. She didn't want to complicate things. Could it be possible that she was a twin? Could Judy Miles be her sister?

Mr. and Mrs. Jackson greeted their daughter with open arms. Ellen had always felt loved and special. They had a leisurely lunch, as Ellen tried to conceal her nervousness. When her father went to lie down, Ellen felt this was the opportunity she had been waiting for. She wanted to wait until she was alone with her mother. Her dad had a heart attack last year and Ellen was fearful of putting any extra stress on him.

"Mom, leave the dishes and come and sit here with me."

Mrs. Jackson could see the concerned look on her daughter's face.

"Is there anything wrong love?"

"Mom I want you to look at this." Ellen handed her the snapshot.

"Oh you look kind of funny in this picture dear."

"Mom this isn't me."

Ellen went on to explain everything that had transpired in the last few weeks. Mrs. Jackson was in tears when Ellen finished.

"Mom I need to know the truth. Was I a twin?"

Mrs. Jackson hesitated momentarily.

"Yes dear you were. You were one of twin girls. Your father and I felt so bad that we couldn't adopt you both."

"Why didn't you ever tell me?" Ellen interrupted.

"You were never interested. Every time I brought up the subject of your adoption you didn't want to hear about it."

Ellen knew her mother was right, she had never asked and didn't care about her biological family. But now she did care. She had a sister, a twin sister. Ellen was now ready to find the answers to the questions she never ventured to ask before.

On Sunday evening she packed her car and headed back to London. Upon leaving, her mother asked what she was going to do.

"I'm going to do the only thing I can do. I'm going to find my sister."

"Be careful dear." Mrs. Jackson understood what her daughter had to do.

"I love you Mom."

The House

I HAVE WALKED PAST it hundreds of times, always wondering who lived there. It is an old, red brick house standing awkwardly amongst strip malls and condos. Everything about it suggests it had been there since the early fifties, but who lived there? An ancient looking TV antenna indicated the owner probably watches television. Maybe the antenna was placed there years ago by a previous owner, but who lives there now? I had never seen anyone other than the landscaping company cutting grass in the summer and shoveling snow in the winter. Maybe it was an old man who had lost his wife, or an old woman who had lost her husband? Maybe it was a young man who had lost his parents in a terrible accident. Maybe it was a millionaire who keeps his money in the house in his mattress! I don't know, but every day when I walk by my mind conjures up a variety of scenarios, some believable and some from a dark place within.

One Sunday morning as I was approaching the house, I noticed a crowd gathering. I tried to push my way through to see what was happening. All I could make out was the flashing lights of an ambulance and a stretcher with paramedics on each side. A body lying on the stretcher was completely covered with a white sheet and being carried down the front steps to be placed into the back of the ambulance. Hushed voices could be heard from people gathering. I tried to listen to what they were saying; did anyone know what had happened? From what I overheard, most people had the same unanswered questions I did. For the rest of the day, I wondered what could have happened. I even walked by the house a couple of times, looking for clues. Dare I walk up the front steps and look through the windows? What if someone was still inside?

The next morning everything appeared quiet and still around the house. With a fresh layer of snow and no foot prints, I knew no one had been about. I walked down the driveway and into the backyard. I was not really sure what I was looking for, but mostly I wanted a clue as to who lived here and who had been taken out on the stretcher. But in the blank snow, no clues were found.

A few days later part of the mystery would be solved. A local newspaper carried the story with the headline "Famous Author Found Dead in Her Home." I quickly began reading. "Successful author, Abigail Stuart, was found dead in her Adelaide Street home, with nearly a million dollars kept in built-in safety deposit boxes. The 99-year-old author of New York Times best sellers such as *Mosh Pit Kids*, *Screaming Voices* and *The People in the Angry House*, was described as a recluse by estranged family members, who say she never accepted the loss of her husband and son in a car accident over 60 years ago. Sources say her son's room was exactly as he left it and her husband's clothes still hung in the closet when investigators entered the house. The safety deposit boxes had been custom built into the walls of the basement. Ms. Stuart's will leaves over a million dollars to local charities."

As a teen, Abigail Stuart was one of my favorite authors. It's hard to believe she was right down the street and lived such an eccentric lifestyle. I guess it's true that you never really know who lives in the house next door.

A Heavenly Christmas

IF YOU COULD HAVE ANOTHER Christmas with your loved ones who have passed, would you? Of course you would. How would that day go? This is how I envision Christmas day with my loved ones who have passed.

As I look out the window, I gaze at the snow gently falling. It is Christmas day and I am filled with excitement and anxiety. The first knock comes and I open the door to see my sister holding her five day old granddaughter Caitlyn, born with Down's syndrome and a serious heart defect. She lived for only five days. My heart fills with so many memories as tears well up and we embrace. Mary's osteoporosis is gone. I am able to hug her without the horrible pain she felt from a simple touch. She appears calm and peaceful. The demons which tormented her mind for the last years of her life seem to have disappeared. She is the happy and healthy sister that I remember from years earlier. Mary had never met Caitlyn in life, but now in heaven was taking care of her until it was time for her mom to come and care for her.

Words are not required as I sit with Mary and Caitlyn until the next knock arrives. I open the door to see my handsome brother with his grandson Josh, and Josh's mother Janet. Lyle is at his best, the edema and cancer gone. We share a moment that I don't believe we ever shared in this mortal world. Josh is handsome, and Janet is beautiful, as they were before their accidents ravaged their bodies and stole their lives. I lead them into the great room where Mary and Caitlyn are sitting. Janet is drawn to Caitlyn. I knew she must be missing her own grandchildren. Mary buries her face in Lyle's chest. The peace on their faces is poignant to see. My feelings intensify as I wonder who would be coming next.

I hear a gentle knock; my breath catches in my throat as I open the door to see two beautiful people standing hand in hand. Mom and Dad look young and healthy, having found their way back to each other in heaven. My eyes begin to burn as tears stream down my face when we embrace. My parents have been gone for so many years that I don't want to let go. In my lifetime I have never seen them together, let alone holding hands. Arm in arm we go into the great room. There are plenty of tears and hugs and love and laughter all around. Again words are not necessary as the heart has its own words, just to be together is enough. I wait for the next tap on the door.

I open the door and see a vaguely familiar face. As he walks into the light I know it is Richard. He is still 17, while I am much older. We hug tightly. I know we are both thinking what our futures would have been if that accident on our first date hadn't taken his life and spared mine. I feel so amazed that he came and that there was still a connection after all these years. We sit together. Words are not needed. Messages seem to magically transfer from one to the other, it is a wondrous experience.

Grandma and Grandpa are next. I knew they would come; they were always there for us. Grandma's perfume triggers memories of family dinners and special gifts. I also knew

Grandpa would like it here, as he was a man of few words. As I guide them into the great room, tears stream down Grandma's face as she sees her family. It had been so long, but the memories were real.

I begin to wonder if Ed would come, then I hear the one last knock on the door. As I open it, my feelings are beyond description. The last eleven years disappear, we are together. He was the man I loved, healthy and happy as I remembered him. The frail, cancer-ridden body is gone. As I close the door behind him, I feel a resistance and there is Rusty, Ginger, and Bob, our pets, pushing their way into the house. My legs felt weak, and I want this day to never end. We both sit on the floor loving our beautiful pets. Everything seems natural and as it should be. Ed and I join the others in the great room. It is so overwhelming to be with all the people I loved so much. There is a peace and joy that I wished would last forever.

Then I hear my grandson calling me. I turn to see my wonderful husband Stan, my sister and her husband, my daughter, my grandchildren and my husband's sons sitting at the dining room table. Stan stands behind an empty chair waiting for me. As I walk toward them I can feel their love drawing me. I know it is not my time. I still have things to do and people to love while on this earth. I look toward the great room and everyone is gone, as if they had never been there, but I know the love will remain alive and in my heart until it is my time.

You probably thought about how your day would be, as I believe most people would be thrilled to have one more day with loved ones who have passed. When my envisioned day came to a close and I joined my earth family I was left with a feeling of peace, and a belief that one day when it was time, I would be with those who had passed. Your day may not be like mine, but unique to you.

Poetry

GRIEF

My world is silenced
I do not hear your voice
I do not feel your touch
Where you sat is empty
Where you slept is empty
You are no more.
My heart aches
My eyes weep
Where are you?
I wait for you
But you do not come.
I want to go to you
But I cannot.
No one would understand.
I have to wait here
Until it is time to be with you again
I hope it will not be too long
As I cannot bear the days and nights of nothingness

A LOYAL COMPANION

The pain in my heart
Must remain in my heart
For if it were known
How my eyes fill with tears
At the mention of your name
Some wouldn't understand.
My days are quieter now
Your voice silenced from the world
As now it only lives within my heart
If others knew
They would laugh
Get over it, they would say
"It was only a dog"
But to me you were so much more.

MADISON

Your beautiful face lights my day
For I cannot imagine a sunrise without you.
Your blue eyes, round and full
Fill me with laughter and tears.
Your fine brown locks
Surround your face.
Your beautiful unlined skin
Soft to the touch.
You are my angel on earth.
I cradle you close
Never wanting to say goodbye.
But tomorrow you will come again.
Gramma! Gramma!

Words to fill my yearning heart.

DEPARTURE

*When they told me you were gone
I felt silent inside.
It had been years since I saw you
But I remember your voice still.
Your unique way of being
Will never be in this life.
Your frail body dissolved
But your infinite soul existing.
An invaluable legacy you have left
For all to see, read, enjoy.
Many will yearn for your guidance
But only those closest will know your true heart.
A fleeting reminder of your extensive spirit
Will live on in the hearts you touched.
Your true essence can never be captured
But will exist for all to strive for.*

Part 3

Excerpt from my unpublished autobiography Can I Come Home Now?

Chapter 1

"AUNT ALICE, WHEN DO you think I'll be able to go home?" Standing in the back, I dangled my arms over the front seat of the car, in the space between Aunt Alice and Uncle George. I saw a look pass between them. As if they knew something I didn't.

"Well, I don't know, Barbara. "It may take your mother and John a long time to work out their problems."

"But it's already been a long time. What kind of problems do they have anyway?"

"It hasn't been that long, just a few months," Aunt Alice replied. She spoke carefully, as if to keep impatience out of her voice. "Anyway, I thought you liked living with us."

"I do, but I still miss my Mom."

There was a pause. Uncle George's eyes were fixed on the long highway ahead. Aunt Alice, too, avoided my eyes. "I wonder if Candy is ready to have her pups yet, what do you think, George?"

I threw myself back on the seat. I hated it when they changed the subject, which they seemed to do whenever I talked about Mom. I was sure they were hiding something from me.

We were on our way back from Windsor to Belle River, a forty-minute drive we made each morning and night, six days a week. Aunt Alice and Uncle George both worked in Windsor, so the Board of Education had given me special permission to attend school in Windsor. I was in grade four. Every morning I walked from Aunt Alice's dry cleaning store to school, then back in the afternoon. Uncle George picked us up around six o'clock and we drove home.

Aunt Alice and Uncle George were really John's uncle and aunt, not mine. John was Mom's boyfriend; he had lived with us for as long as I could remember. My own father lived a few blocks away from us. I couldn't remember his living with us before he and Mom separated.

Uncle George was in his fifties and didn't have much hair left. When he smiled I could see the few stubby teeth that remained. He had never been married before he met Aunt Alice; they had been together ten years now. Aunt Alice had been in one other marriage. On her dresser was a picture of a baby boy, her only child, who had died in infancy. When I asked her about the picture her voice became unusually soft, and I could see the sadness in her eyes.

There were many good things about living with Uncle George and Aunt Alice. They lived in the country on the banks of the Ruscom River, in a two-bedroom white-frame bungalow they were building themselves. It wasn't finished, which created some practical problems but, still, I had my own room, all the food I could ever want, and my own dog, a black poodle named Gypsy.

It was certainly different from living with Mom and John. John was seven years younger than Mom, and when he came to live with us my oldest brother Lyle seemed to resent his presence the most. The two of them began fighting almost from the first day, and the fights soon became physical. The night John kicked Lyle out of the house was an evening that Lyle had been left in charge of Mary and me. Mom and John had gone out for the evening. My older sister Jeanne was usually our babysitter, but she was over at a friend's.

Lyle invited a few of his buddies over, and then a few more. Eventually it turned into a party, and Mary and I, who were five and four, spent the evening trying to stay out of the way of the drunken teenagers. We were so glad to see Mom and John when they finally came home.

But when John spotted Lyle, lying semi-conscious in a chair, he reached down, grabbed him by the shirt, and pulled him to his feet.

"What the hell is going on here?" John's huge eyes were black with anger. I had seen that anger before. Mary and I hid behind Mom.

Lyle looked confused. He tried to focus on John's face.

"Answer me, you goddamn' idiot!"

Mom tried to pull John's hands off Lyle. "Leave him alone, John. He doesn't understand what you're saying."

"You keep your nose out of this. I pay the bills around here, not this hoodlum son of yours."

Still holding Lyle, John yelled at the others. "You'd better all get the hell out of here before I call the police."

Mom came over and clutched Mary and I tightly in her arms. John's voice was scary, and we were glad to be somewhere safe. The house emptied in minutes.

Lyle was sobering up quickly; he tried to pull away from John. "Leave me alone!"

John wasn't much taller than Lyle, but he lifted weights and was a street fighter, while Lyle was still a lanky teenager.

"Sure, kid, I'll leave you alone." He dragged Lyle to the back door. Lyle managed to shake him off, but John grabbed him again, this time getting a better grip.

Mom, who had let Mary and me go, was screaming at John. "Let him go, you're going to hurt him!"

John ignored her and pushed Lyle out the back door. "Don't you ever come back or you'll wish you hadn't."

Lyle banged at the door. "Ma, let me in, please Ma!"

Mom moved to open the door.

"Millie, if you touch that door I'll leave and never come back."

"But he's my son; I can't just leave him out there."

I couldn't bear to see the tears pouring from her eyes.

"You heard what I said, it's him or me."

Mom turned away from the door and ran to the bathroom. We could hear her weeping until Lyle stopped banging. Then an awful silence descended.

John went to the bathroom and tried to turn the handle. "Come on, Millie, open the door." His voice was cajoling now. When he heard the click of the lock he opened the door and took Mom into his arms.

"Cheer up, we did the best thing. That boy has got to grow up; he'll thank us for this one day."

Mom gave in to John's caresses. I was sad Lyle was gone but glad the fight was over, glad to see them hugging. I wanted to rush in and hug them too, but I knew John would only push me away.

In the 1950s it was the law that if a separated woman was living with a man she was not married to, her ex-husband didn't have to pay child support. Dad had stopped paying child support as soon as he'd found out about John. Unfortunately, the welfare office also clued in, and cut off the monthly payments. I remember John rationing our food and being hungry a lot.

When I was five years old Mom registered Mary and me at King Edward Public School. Mary was a year older than me but hadn't started school the previous year because kindergarten wasn't mandatory. Now she was put into grade one, while I went into kindergarten. Mary didn't like going to school and didn't see why she should have to go all day when I had to go only in the morning. Every day after lunch she yelled and stomped her feet until Mom let her stay home. On the days Mom was strong and made her go back, Mary came home after school with soiled underwear.

Finally John stepped in. One day, when Mary and I came in after school John noticed Mary's odd way of walking and called her over to him. She started towards him, but he grabbed her hand and pulled her into the living room. Then he called the rest of us in.

"You might all learn something," he said. He began to take off Mary's clothing. He took the pants that were full of faeces and rubbed them all over her naked body. I watched in horror.

I could see Mary's shoulders quivering. I wanted to yell at John to stop but I was afraid. He made her stand in the corner covered in faeces, with the rest of us reluctantly watching.

Jeanne ignored John's threats and ran out of the house. The next day Grandma and Grandpa rushed down and took Mary away to live with them on their farm just outside Windsor. Mary had always been Grandma's favourite. She had spent many holidays and weekends with Grandma, Grandpa, and Mom's only brother, Uncle Jack, who still lived at home. Aside from her stubbornness, Mary was a quiet, content girl whom Grandma and Grandpa could manage even at their age. Mom didn't seem to put up much of a fuss as she packed Mary's clothes into cardboard boxes. I was devastated.

"I wish you could stay here, Mary."

"I don't want to anyway, because of what John did to me."

We hugged and kissed good-bye and I gave her a picture of me. She promised to bring one for me the next time she came to visit. I was quickly getting the message not to cross John, or I might be the next to go.

It was Jeanne who left next. She moved in with Dad when she couldn't take fighting with Mom and John any more. There were just the three of us now and the house felt empty. I wished everyone would come back home. If I asked Mom when Mary was coming back she always said the same thing: "Some day dear, some day we will all be together again."

By this time, we lived in the east end of Windsor, just before a viaduct on Hill Street, which was well known for the delinquents and good-for-nothings it spawned at that time. The house, a bungalow, had been painted at one time, but now it was just old bare wood that was cracked and dried out. Outside was a big backyard, where John parked his car. The weeds grew wildly around it. The front of the house was surrounded by a hedge that was almost as high as the roof. John wouldn't let anyone trim the hedge; he said it gave us privacy.

Each window in the house had a green roll-up blind covering it, all of them—under John's orders—kept pulled down. Sometimes during the day Mom opened them. It felt wonderful to see the sun beaming in for a few hours.

John had many other rules that Mom and I had to obey. We were not allowed to answer the door. If someone knocked, John would go into the front bedroom and peek out through the edge of the blind to see who was there. If he didn't recognize the person, which was most of the time, he would tell Mom and I to stay perfectly still and not move a muscle until the knocking stopped. When I asked John why we had to do this he laughed nervously. He always laughed when people asked him a question.

The phone was the same way. He let it ring, maybe ten times, and then he'd pick up the receiver. He wouldn't say anything until the other person spoke. If he recognized the voice he would talk, if not he hung up.

Gradually I learned to keep out of John's way and do what he wanted. I forced myself to eat all my vegetables and everything else on my plate. I tried not to talk back to him or Mom. I didn't answer the door or the phone. The worst thing I had to do was sit on his lap and let him tickle me. As long as I did all these things, we got along fine. Sometimes he would give me a pocket full of coins to spend on whatever I wanted. I began to even like him and to see him as a father—I knew him better than I knew Dad.

After Jeanne and Mary left, John and Mom began drinking and fighting more and more often. I hated the screaming and the things that got thrown. I couldn't stand to see John hitting Mom. When I tried to stop them, John ordered me to my room. This was almost worse than the fighting. I never went there until I absolutely had to, at bedtime; it was always dark because of the pulled-down blinds, and Mom couldn't convince me there weren't monsters in the closet. Every corner had a dark moving shadow. When the shouting got louder and closer, I took refuge under Mary's old bed. I folded my hands in prayer the way Grandma had shown me and squeezed my eyes shut. Because it was so dark anyway I couldn't tell when it was time for bed. On these nights I knew no one would come in to kiss me good night or tuck me in. Eventually I fell asleep under the bed with my clothes on.

The fights became a regular occurrence. I couldn't understand how Mom and John could hug and kiss so passionately before John left for work, and then, by the time they got home in the evening, usually after drinking in one of the hotels, be fighting with equal passion.

The mornings after were always the same. When I got up, sore from the hard floor, the house was a mess of broken dishes and other objects. Mom was silently cleaning up, her eyes red and swollen. Her wrists were bruised from John's grip. We didn't say anything to each other; I went around and picked up the larger pieces of debris, careful not to cut myself, until it was time for school.

It was during the summer holidays after I finished grade one that Mom arranged for me to spend a few weeks with Dad and Jeanne. I hardly knew Dad. The only previous contact we had that I remembered was when Jeanne was still living at home and I used to tag along when she met him for dinner on Friday nights. I thought he was a nice-looking man. He always wore a hat and a white shirt, as well as dark pants held up by suspenders. His skin was pale and his eyes a soft blue. He wasn't very tall. If I lost him in a crowd I could never see his head, so I looked for his shoes. He had fallen arches and had to have his shoes specially made, so they were always the same style: black or brown lace-up oxfords that squeaked when he walked.

Dad and Jeanne were living on the upper floor of a small building that housed four two-bedroom apartments. The apartment had all the necessary furniture, yet it still felt empty; there were no pictures on the walls or shelves of knickknacks like at Mom's.

Jeanne was eighteen now and working in a nearby store as a cashier. She had quit school before finishing grade twelve but was planning on going back to finish someday soon. She was dating a boy named Greg.

I enjoyed my visit, but looked forward to going home to Mom. When it was about time for me to leave, though, Jeanne and Dad told me Mom was sick and wouldn't be able to take care of me, and that I'd have to stay with them for awhile. I tried to argue that I could take care of myself, and asked if I could at least call Mom, but Jeanne told me she was in the hospital with pneumonia.

I reluctantly resigned myself for a long stay. Fortunately Dad lived in the same school district as Mom, so I could attend the same school and keep the same friends. Still, after about a month I became anxious to see Mom. I hadn't heard a word from her.

One night at dinner I got up the courage to tell Dad how I felt. "Daddy, I want to call Mom and see if she's better yet, okay?"

My question obviously took him by surprise. He stopped eating and gave me a stunned look.

"Please, Daddy, I really miss her."

"Okay, Barbara," he said finally, "we'll see what we can do." I was immediately cheered—I even missed John. I was worried they had left me the way Mary and Lyle had. The next afternoon while Dad was at work Jeanne and I tried to phone Mom but the number had been disconnected. We searched through the phone book but there were no listings under either Mom's name or John's.

I became hysterical. "What if Mom has died! Oh I know that's what's happened. I'll never be able to see her again!"

"Stop it! Stop it!" Jeanne shouted. "Mom has not died. She probably just doesn't have a phone. Tomorrow when I get home from work I'll take you over to see her, okay?"

I felt immediately better, but my relief was short-lived: someone else was living in our old house on Hill Street. I began thinking horrible things had happened to Mom and started blubbering uncontrollably.

"Stop this right now!" Jeanne yelled. But I could see she was upset too. "Mom is not dead. If she had died someone would have told us. You just have to face it, Barbara, she doesn't care about us—otherwise she would have told us where she'd moved to."

"Why doesn't she care?" I didn't want to hear this. It couldn't be true.

"I think John has a lot to do with it. When you're older you'll understand more. But don't forget we've still got Dad."

I didn't really feel like I did have Dad. I never knew what to talk to him about or even how to act around him. He worked, as he had since he was eighteen, at Ford Motor Company as a lift truck driver. When he wasn't on evening shifts he fell asleep in front of the TV, his breath was so heavy with the smell of liquor I could smell it across the room. When I kissed him good night the smell made my stomach queasy.

He was not very demonstrative, with either Jeanne or me. His main gesture of affection was to walk by me, put one hand on my head, then hit it with the other and laugh.

I missed Mom's hugs.

One night I woke up to find Dad sitting on my bed with his arm around me.

"Its okay, Barbara," he murmured, "its okay."

I didn't know what was okay, but I enjoyed his arm around me in the darkness.

In the morning he told me I'd been screaming and crying in my sleep and must have been having a nightmare. It came back to me then: I'd been dreaming about Mom—I kept reaching for her but she moved farther and farther away. I didn't tell Dad or Jeanne my dream, but I had it many times and often woke to find Dad at my bedside.

Jeanne was increasingly finding it a burden to look after me, especially, when I interfered with her social life. Occasionally she vented her frustration at Dad. "She's not my kid, why should I have to take care of her?"

"I'm sorry," Dad pleaded, "But what else can I do?"

I felt more and more as though I didn't belong there. Jeanne was constantly yelling at me to do this or that, and when her friends were over I was not allowed to stay in the same room.

"If you don't get out of here right now," Jeanne threatened, I'll tell Dad not to buy you anything on Friday."

I left, although I knew Dad would still buy me anything I wanted. Friday evenings or Saturday mornings, depending on his shift, were our shopping expeditions to the market downtown.

I looked forward to this time. There was always so much happening, so much to see. Everyone was a salesman trying to convince those passing by that his produce was the freshest. Before we went home Dad usually went into a certain store by himself, making me stand around the corner. He said children weren't allowed in these stores. He came out with a brown paper bag that he tried to hide under his arm.

"What's that, Daddy?"

"Oh, never mind, it's nothing for you to concern yourself with." He clutched my hand and held his head high, as I often saw him do, his eyes focused straight ahead.

When we got home and he had gone into another room, I peeked into the bag to see the bottle of whiskey. I wondered why he kept it a secret. Mom and John never hid their bottles.

I had never stopped thinking about Mom. I knew she would want me back if only I could find her. I missed her more and more each day. It had been almost a year since I had come to live with Dad and Jeanne, a year since I'd seen Mom. I was scared that maybe she really was dead and nobody wanted to tell me. If I asked Dad or Jeanne about her they made vague replies and changed the subject.

Finally the day I always longed for came. Grandma and Grandpa called to say they would be over to visit Jeanne and me. When they arrived, they took us out to dinner and told us Mom was feeling better and wanted to see us. Jeanne didn't see why we should be bothered with her, but I grabbed the piece of paper with the address on it and the next afternoon after school went to find Mom. I didn't tell Jeanne or Dad, afraid they wouldn't let me go.

Mom and John had moved into a smaller house, just two streets over from Hill Street. I walked up the laneway and knocked on the door. I hoped Grandma had given me the correct house number. I knocked and knocked. Finally I saw the blind move and the door quickly opened. At last I felt my mother's arms around me.

"Oh my Barbara, I have missed you so much."

I couldn't stop crying. I couldn't say anything. I just wanted to stay in her arms forever.

After we calmed ourselves, Mom gave me cookies and milk and invited me to stay for supper. In the meantime, John had come home and seemed happy to see me.

After supper I helped Mom clean up the kitchen. "Do you want John to drive you home now?" she asked, glancing at the clock. It was seven.

Tears filled my eyes. "I don't want to go; I want to stay here with you."

Mom was silent. Then she put her arms around me. "Barbara, I want you to stay too, honey, but I have nothing to give, not even a bed."

"I'll sleep on the floor, please Mom." Her eyes softened.

We went to a phone booth to call Dad.

Jeanne answered, furious when she heard it was Mom. I could hear her voice even from where I was standing. "I had a feeling she was with you, the least you could have done was call us, we were worried sick. Bring her home right now."

"Barbara doesn't want to stay with you and your father; she wants to live with me." Mom's words sounded mean, and it wasn't true I didn't want to live with them; it was just that I wanted to live with Mom. And since Mom had legal custody of me, there was nothing Dad or Jane could do.

I began Grade 3 at the same school but from yet another home. My friends thought it was weird the way I moved from one house to another, from one parent to another. None of them had divorced parents.

I had forgotten about Mom and John's fights while I'd been away, but I was soon enough reacquainted. What was worse than the fighting was if the door was locked and no one answered the door when I arrived home after school. Usually it was dark by the time they got home and I was so relieved to see them I'd forget to be angry.

One evening I was sitting on the porch, hoping they would come home before it got dark. The dark outside was worse than in my room. The familiar street disappeared and strange old white-haired men who coughed a lot and swayed from side to side shuffled past the house. It got later and later and still they hadn't come. I was getting frantic. Finally, an aunt of John's who lived down the street saw me sitting on the porch.

"Come with me, Barbara; we'll leave a note for your mother." Her voice was sharp, but it didn't seem to be directed towards me. She had taken me in on a couple of other occasions, making a bed for me on the floor in the living room.

When Mom came for me the next day, she apologized to Aunt Rosie and said it wouldn't happen again. Aunt Rosie's expressionless face looked from Mom to me, then away. She had heard this before.

Another evening Mom and John were going out and said I could sleep in their bed until they got home. I loved sleeping in Mom's bed. I felt warm and secure. I crawled into the bed and wrapped the covers tightly around myself.

About an hour later John came back, evidently having forgotten something. When he turned on the light from the kitchen it shone into the bedroom. I wasn't asleep, although my eyes were closed. I could feel John standing nearby. I pulled the covers down from my face and saw him there, staring at me with a silly look on his face.

"Not sleeping yet, eh?" He sat on the side of the bed. "You're such a pretty girl, you know that? You're almost as pretty as your mother."

I laughed nervously. He rubbed the side of my face for a few moments, then left. I felt funny for a while afterwards.

On Thursdays I rushed home from school to see Grandma and Grandpa, who came to visit every other week because Grandma belonged to a bridge club in town. Mary came with them if she had a holiday from school. It seemed as if every time

I saw Grandma she made the same comment: "You are so wild, Barbara, your mother must have gone to a circus when she was pregnant with you."

I tried to be like Mary while Grandma was visiting. I tried to sit still and be quiet but it was hard, and I could never be still enough to win her approval.

Grandma was a beautiful lady, her skin smooth and unlined. She wore a fur coat, which felt soft when she hugged me. Her cheeks were rosy from a touch of rouge, and her lips were a soft red. She wore no other make-up. I loved the smell of her perfume, and sometimes she would put a dab on my wrist. I tried to avoid washing that spot until every trace of the scent had vanished.

Grandpa was the typical strong, silent male. He was a handsome man, with pronounced cheekbones and a thick head of red hair, which Mom and I had inherited. His voice was gruff and hard for me to understand. Grandma, however, was ever ready to repeat his words.

Often Grandma brought me hand-me-downs from Mary, and sometimes she gave me money or candy. For Mom she brought homemade jams and fruit. Then she would start on Mom about John.

"I don't know why you're staying here with that man. He's no better than your husband. You should bring all the children to live with your father and me. We'll keep you together as a family."

"Ma, I have to live my own life."

"Mildred, stop thinking of yourself and do something for the sake of your children—they need a home."

Mom invariably became upset and began to cry. I went to her and put my arm around her shoulder. She held my other hand tightly.

"Okay, okay, I'll think about it."

Even though I got mad at Grandma for making Mom cry, I secretly hoped we could go to live at Grandma and Grandpa's and all be together.

After I went to live with Uncle George and Aunt Alice, it was Uncle George I came to see as my father. He was playful and spry for his age and for his size—he had an enormous stomach. From the time I was quite young—when we used to visit before I lived there—he chased me around the yard and, when he caught me, threw me on the ground and tickled me. We played a game with his stomach.

"Here, Barbara, you want to see some magic?"

"Yeah."

"Okay, press my belly button really hard."

I pressed it with my index finger until it was perfectly flat. His tongue came out and I giggled. Then he motioned for me to watch his hands. He put one up to his left ear and pretended to turn the ear. This caused the tongue slowly to go back into his mouth. Then he turned the other ear and his belly popped back out. This trick fascinated me when I was four or five, but by the time I was nine, I had it figured out.

I loved being with Uncle George—he was fun and he didn't look at me and laugh in the strange way that John sometimes had.

With Aunt Alice, I was less comfortable. I think it was because Mom didn't like her. I felt I would be betraying Mom if I liked Aunt Alice too much. She was a large-framed and fair-skinned woman—of German ancestry, though she rarely talked about her roots. She was only in her mid fifties, but her hair had been completely white for almost as long as I could remember. She wore no make-up except for ruby red lipstick; but even this didn't last long because she was forever licking her lips.

She seemed to have two different personalities: one for company and one for home. When she was with others, she was friendly and laughed at everything that was remotely funny. At home she was serious and miserable. I hardly ever saw her laugh; mostly she barked out orders for Uncle George and spent the rest of the time criticizing me. I tried to stay out of her way as much as possible.

Afterword

I hope you enjoyed reading this book. I would appreciate it if you could take the time to give me a rating or review on your favorite book site.

Feel free to send comments about this book or my previous book, Dear Barb: Answers to Your Everyday Questions- to my email at barbgodin53@gmail.com.

Follow my webpage barbgodin.com for the release of my next book and to read more of my writing.

Don't miss out!

Visit the website below and you can sign up to receive emails whenever BARBARA GODIN publishes a new book. There's no charge and no obligation.

https://books2read.com/r/B-A-EPYK-QIQLB

BOOKS 2 READ

Connecting independent readers to independent writers.

Did you love *Glimpses in Time: A Collection of Memoirs and More*? Then you should read *Dear Barb: Answers to Your Everyday Questions*[1] by BARBARA GODIN!

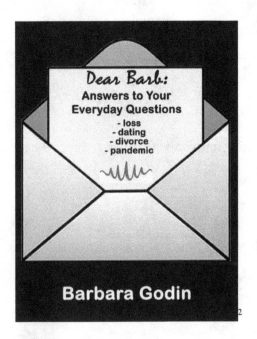

Dear Barb: Answers to Your Everyday Questions
    By Barbara Godin
    Do you sometimes feel like you need a second opinion, but you don't want to tell anyone what's going on in your life? "Dear Barb: Answers to Your Everyday Questions" provides a common sense approach to dealing with many of the issues of daily life. For example, Dana is intimately involved with both of her roommates and her exboyfriend wants to reconcile, what

1. https://books2read.com/u/brWZZZ

2. https://books2read.com/u/brWZZZ

does she do? Patty doesn't know what to do since she feels she's in a marriage of three? Jessica's mom is downsizing and wants Jessica to take all her stuff, Jessica doesn't want her mom's stuff, how does she tell her mom without hurting her feelings? Big Red wants to know if it's all right to watch porn. Pat put his dog down and now he has second thoughts about whether he made the right decision. Melinda lost her younger brother to cancer and doesn't know how to move on without him. These are some of the questions included in "Dear Barb: Answers to your Everyday Questions."

Barbara Godin has been answering questions since 2003 when she responded to a call for an advice columnist for The Voice Magazine. Barbara submitted a sample column and was chosen as the new advice columnist. Barbara had always been the" go to person" for her friends. A difficult life provided her with the experience to be able to write over 500 Dear Barb columns and ultimately create a book that everyone can relate to.

Most people will be able to find themselves somewhere in the pages of "Dear Barb: Answers to your Everyday Questions." Dear Barb is an easy read and would also make a great gift for a friend or family member who is going through a difficult time.

Read more at www.barbgodin.com.

Also by BARBARA GODIN

Dear Barb: Answers to Your Everyday Questions
Glimpses in Time: A Collection of Memoirs and More

Watch for more at www.barbgodin.com.

About the Author

Barbara Godin is the author of *Dear Barb: Answers to Your Everyday Questions*. She continues to write her *Dear Barb* column www.voicemagazine.org and other short stories. Barbara's latest book is *Glimpses in Time: A Collection of Memoirs and More*. Barbara lives in Chatham Ontario with her husband Stan and their dog Suzie. Visit Barbara's web site at barbgodin.com. Barbara is also on Facebook, Instagram and Twitter@BarbGod. Feel free to email comments to barbgodin53@gmail.com.

Read more at www.barbgodin.com.